Shattered Dreams and Broken Hearts

By Rev. Michael Shaw

With Victoria Lee

Edited by
Edward A. Clark, Lieutenant Colonel, USAF Retired

Copyright 1995 Victoria Lee
All rights reserved, this book, or parts thereof,
may not be reproduced in any form without permission.

Preassigned LCCN: 95-61996
ISBN 1-888225-00-9

Published by

A Touch of Heart
P.O. Box 470212
Tulsa, Oklahoma 74147-0212

To My Beautiful and very
Special Wife

Rosemary

and to our children

Aaron, Carrieann, Damon,
Christi, Rachel

and to all of our friends
who helped make
this book a reality.

REVIEW AND SUPPORT CREDIT

Kimberlee Clark

Cara Cook

P.J. Gardner

TABLE OF CONTENTS

Preface	5
Introduction	9
A Time of Youth	11
Covered by the Blood	20
A Shattered Dream	37
The Anointing and the Calling	51
All Things Are Possible, If You Only Believe	61
Let Go And Let God	83
Joy Comes in the Morning	93
It's Not The End, It's Just the Beginning	119
Broken Hearts	137
Darkest, Just Before The Dawn	149
Victory Prevails	163
Let the Redeemed of the Lord, Say So	176

PREFACE

*"It's not what people do not say about you that hurts,
but what they say, that you know is not true!"*

When was the last time that you experienced a broken heart from a bad relationship or a marriage that had gone sour. And, how many times have you felt like giving up on the dreams and hopes that you spent years working on?

Maybe it was this morning when you found out that things just got worse instead of better in your life. Maybe it was last night when you went to bed and while laying there all alone, you decided that life was just not worth living any longer. Or maybe it started years ago as a child or teenager and you have spent many years just coasting along and praying that things would get better. If any of these apply, then this book is definitely for you! For you are not alone in your failures and mistakes and it's alright to realize that you should be doing much better. You have a right to scream out at the world and to God and say, "I've Blown It or I've Made Mistakes Lord and I Need Help!"

Your success in life depends on your ability to recognize and overcome your shortcomings, failures and mistakes. For there is little wrong with failing as long as you realize that you made a mistake and you failed and it's time to go on and make a change from where you are in life to where you want to be.

When preparing for this book, many emotions were running through my mind. What would people think and most of all, how would they feel and react to another testimony or biography about someone that they didn't even know or had never met, yet who had gone through similar circumstances in their life.

There have been many books written on positive thinking and prosperity and how important it is to live right for the Lord. Yet when was the last time that you read a book about Christians making mistakes and having failures and struggling in their life to serve the Lord. Everytime I think about the 11th Chapter of Hebrews in the Bible, I am reminded that everyone mentioned in that chapter, which is called the great "Faith" chapter, had blown it and made many mistakes in their lives. But, they all had one thing in common, they never gave up and they learned how to walk in victory with the Lord.

I've learned that being a Christian doesn't mean that you won't sin or fail or make mistakes in life. In fact the real battle does not begin until you become a Christian. Making mistakes and failing in life, all too often happens too easily, but if you are a Christian, that should help you in the recovery process. Because success very often depends on the Christian principles of picking yourself up when you fall down and learning from your mistakes. But, most of all it means walking in obedience to the things of the Lord.

Following in the footsteps of Jesus will not always be easy but it will be rewarding. He will never leave you or forsake you during your time of trouble. However, you must learn how to trust him in every area and circumstance of your life.

The life of Jesus was more than just performing miracles and ministering to people. When His life is looked at closely, it reveals much of the same pain and hurt that each of us face. He knew what it felt like to be alone, even in a crowd. He knew the pain of betrayal by those that He loved. He knew what it was like to be popular one day and hated the next. And, He knew that the nature of people was to forget today about those things that you did for them yesterday. Especially, when they are confronted with the fact that you are in trouble or have failed in some way.

Maybe you have never experienced the Lord or met Him, but I can tell you from experience, that He is real. He wants to be a part of your life even now in the midst of your most difficult situations and problems. And what you will experience will be the most overwhelming flow of love that you have ever known. Therefore, as I share my own personal trials, tribulations and eventual triumphs, I pray that if you see a reflection of yourself from time to time that you will realize that no matter what you are facing in life, there are answers to your-

"SHATTERED DREAMS AND BROKEN HEARTS".

INTRODUCTION

For over five years, I have worked on this book and I have endeavored to see it released, especially during what seemed to be the most difficult times of my life. For the past year, I have tried on many occasions to see this book become a reality, instead of just a dream.

A couple of times we would raise the money for the production only to have something come up and again face a time of set back on the date of release. Then, we would have to return the money that had been invested and we were back to square one again.

There were those who constantly told others that this book would never be released. Yet the miracle that a number of people thought would never come to pass, is now a reality.

There are many people today that are facing some kind of hurt or pain or even disability in their life. Try as we may, none of us will ever escape the trials of life or the pain and suffering that comes to each of us in time. Yet we must realize that in spite of the Shattered Dreams and Broken Hearts there is someone that really cares for you. His name is JESUS.

<u>Remember</u>, that with Him your dreams and miracles are very often just one step away!

Staring at the reflection in the window, I could hardly recognize the individual that was staring back at me. I thought I had known this person and yet he seemed different. Gone was the joy and happiness that had been a part of my life and expressions which had touched the lives of millions of people through television, radio or crusades. Gone was the strong bass and baritone voice that had sung to millions and ministered the Word of God. Gone was the special anointing that had been given by the Holy Spirit and had touched people from all backgrounds......

***

"Train up a child

in the way he should go

and when he is old,

he will not depart from it."

Proverbs 22:6

"Let no man despise thy youth,

but be thou an example of the believers

in word, conversation, in love,

in spirit, in faith, in purity."

1 Timothy 4:12

***

Chapter One

A TIME FOR YOUTH

"Oh Ralph look at him, isn't he the most precious little boy you've ever seen? I love it when he smiles and his eyes are such a bright baby blue. And look at his cute little fingers and toes. Each one is so perfectly shaped. Look at his little head Ralph. I think he looks just like you. Let's call him Michael."

There I was all 8 pounds and 13 ounces of healthy boy. And mom made sure everyone knew it. It was a cold winter day in Decatur, Illinois when I decided to make my well announced arrival. And I've been making my presence known ever since.

I wish I could say, those first few days of pure joy over my arrival filled my family home with continued happiness. But, the truth is the Williams home was far from being happy. My biological father and mother Evelyn shared two other children, my oldest sister Linda and my other sister Gloria. We little ones were all about two years apart in age. So, mom had her hands full with two beautiful, bouncy, little delicate girls and one rambunctious rowdy boy. My father was a good man and he loved us. But, somehow he had a problem with gambling that he just couldn't seem to quit. To him it was just a way of life. He just couldn't seem to realize that it was destroying his family right before his eyes. Until one day, it was just too late. Poor mom worked so hard to keep our family together. But everytime we'd get a little bit of money my father would squander it somewhere gambling. It seemed to be a never ending cycle. Of course at the time I didn't really understand. Things were always left a little sketchy in our minds, because we were never allowed to discuss the problems that we were having in our home. We just knew that mom was unhappy and for some reason things just were not right. Neither mom or my father were Christians so they didn't even have that to hang on to when the times got rough. One Memorial Day after returning home from a family visit in Southern Illinois, my father was outside pushing my sister Linda on the swing while Gloria and I played nearby. He said,

"Kids, I have to go to California for a while on business, but I will be back soon."

You could tell by the look on her face that Linda was not buying that little speech one bit. She knew he wasn't telling the truth and she confronted him about it. She said,

"Please don't go, I know you're not coming back."

Sometimes we don't give our children enough credit for being sensitive to the atmosphere around them. But my father swore to her that he would return. As expected though, when he did return from his trip two weeks later, Linda's fears began to play themselves out. Mom went into Linda's room and announced that our father and her were not going to live together any longer.

"Linda, you are going to have to choose which one of us that you are going to live with."

Linda turned to mom and said,

"What did Michael and Gloria decide to do mom?"

With tears in her eyes she replied,

"They have decided to go with your father."

He came into the room at that moment holding me and Gloria in his arms and said to mom,

"What has Linda decided to do?"

As she proceeded to tell him about Linda's decision, you could tell that it was making him angry, but he agreed that it would be better if all the children stayed together. So reluctantly he told mom that she could keep us. The whole ordeal was so sad and tragic because he truly did love mom. There was something inside of him that wouldn't allow him to lay aside his hurtful lifestyle. Mom had taken all of the abuse she could. She felt that somehow there had to be a life out there that was better for us than the one we were experiencing.

I remember the last time I saw my father we were standing outside one of the local pool halls that he frequently visited. He was saying his last good-byes. I'll never forget how he knelt down in front of me, a little four year old boy (that wanted to be just like his father) and said,

"Son you're the man of the house now. It's up to you to take good care of your mom and sisters."

What a devastating remark to make to a young impressionable little boy. Truly a day I will never forget. It was 16 years later before I ever spoke to him again.

***

Mom was a beautiful and caring woman so it wasn't long before she met a man, Eugene Shaw who was soon to sweep her off her feet. It didn't take them long to decide they wanted to spend the rest of their lives together. So they were married and we moved to Michigan City, Indiana. Then as God would have it, I was joined by another bubbly female. Mom and Eugene became the proud parents of a little baby girl named Debbie. And, sometime later there was the arrival of a second little girl whom we called Robin. The Shaw family was then made up of Mom, Dad and five children. My older sisters and I took on the Shaw name. It seemed more appropriate and less confusing for us all to do that especially since my biological father was no longer in the picture. Of course back in the "50's" it was less common than it is now to see divorced families. So, it just made it less traumatic for everyone if we all shared the same last name. That way hopefully an outsider would be less likely to dissect us into two separate parts.

Being a child that has come from a broken dysfunctional home certainly has its share of scars. But, don't we all - in one form or the other. Even in the best of homes we all carry with us a degree of mistakes and ill-judgements. What I dislike about that is we sometimes use our past to justify our failures of the future. Instead, we should be taking those scars and mistakes and using them as guidelines or character builders. But too often, too many of us allow them to keep us from becoming the best that we can be.

As a four year old boy, that remembered vividly staring into the eyes of his father, as he said his farewell and being told that he was now the man of the house, I experienced further adjustments to then find that another man was taking his place. But time was on our side and eventually I was ready to relate to my mom's new husband and before long accept him as my dad. Oh we've had our ups and downs over the years that's for sure. There were times when I didn't think he would ever understand me. But as the years have gone, so has our inability to communicate. And now we have a relationship that is beginning to heal with time and the help of the Lord. There have been many times in my life where I have looked back on my childhood days and thought of all the good times. Times when I was free to just be a kid. When all I had to think about was playing outside with my friends. I remember living on my grandfather's farm and playing outside until the very last minute. And, mom would then yell at us from the back door that it was time to come in and get ready for supper. Many times I would try and eat quickly with dad telling me to slow down and take my time. He said there would be plenty of time to play and be with my friends. Then after being excused I would hurry outside and hope that they were still waiting. Yet many times they would have all gone home and I found myself alone. When that happened, I would make my way to the small woods at the back of the house. At my favorite spot I would lay down on a blanket that I had taken out of my bedroom. I would watch the sunset and then watch the stars and moon come out. With anticipation I would lay there hoping I would see a shooting star that I could wish upon before my parents called me in for the evening. I was continually making wishes about what I would one day do with my life.

Quite often, I have wondered what Jesus dreamed about and what He wished for as a small boy. His childhood was just like yours and mine and there were things that He wanted to do when He got older as well. He knew that there would come a day when He would have to fulfill His Father's plan, but until then, I believe that He would dream and hope just like you and me.

I had many dreams about my life and many thoughts and never once did any of them include being a minister of the gospel or even a singer. I can still hear my mother's voice when she would sing to us as children and when she would tuck me in at night. She would always ask if I had said my prayers and sometimes even wait until I was through praying before she left the room. I still frequently think of those words she would say to me as a child, in which she would then remind me that I had plenty of time to make decisions for my life. Also, that it was alright to make mistakes because that is how you learn.

She used to sing a song to us as children titled, "Casa rah, sa rah, whatever will be, will be!" Yet I learned as I got older that each of us will decide our own future and what we will become by whether or not we really want it in life. Your tomorrow is just one step away and your childhood can be a stepping stone or a hindrance to your future.

As parents we should never let our children lose out on their tomorrow by cheating them out of their childhood today! It's important now to take a stand in your child's life. As a parent, you can still control what they watch and where they go and who they spend their time with. You can also participate in what they are being taught in school. Yet we must all realize that the devil and the world are constantly trying to take control of our child's life. And, that there will come a day, when our children will have the opportunity to make their own decisions. Also, it will be then, that as parents we can leave them in the hands of God, knowing that they were taught well as children.

***

"That if thou shalt confess with thy mouth

the Lord Jesus,

and shalt believe in thine heart

that God hath raised him from the dead,

thou shalt be saved.

For with the heart man believeth

unto righteousness;

and with the mouth confession is made

unto salvation.

For whosoever shall call upon the name of

the Lord,

shall be saved.

Romans 10:9,10,13

Chapter Two

COVERED BY THE BLOOD

After Mom married Eugene we moved to Indiana where we lived two houses down from his brother. Uncle Kenny had four daughters who then became my cousins. They were Kayla, Denise, Anita and Margie and we were all pretty close to the same age. So, a lot of hours were spent with them while we all explored new adventures and ideas. I bet anyone of them could come up with some amazing stories about the great exploits we all experienced together.

My good friend Don Gifford moved onto our street with his mom and dad and brother Jerry when I was only eight years old. Childhood buddies can be some of the most memorable people in our lives. That time of our life is when we are just beginning to experience true relationships and learning how to inter-act with another person other than our parents or siblings. For, in this relationship, that is not always guarded by adult supervision, you have many hours of learning how to communicate with each other as a peer of great influence. And if you are fortunate your influence on each other is a positive thing. I've got memories of Don that can never be erased. As we both serve the Lord in ministry we've had our differences, but he will always be my best friend in life. I've always learned that a friend will be there during the bad times as well as the good times. Don's friendship became more important to me after the experience we shared, where he saved me from what could have been a fatal accident and then later in life when he was there during the death of my mother.

When I turned ten years old dad and mom decided to move to a little community called Three Oaks, Michigan. It was a beautiful place with a population of only 1800 people. If you worked at it, it wouldn't take long before you would be able to know everyone in town.

Shortly after arriving there I started my own paper route. That made me one of the lucky ones because it gave me the opportunity to meet a majority of those 1800 friendly neighbors. One of my stops was always at the local Rexall Drugstore where our pharmacist Mr. Gimber spent most of his days. Mr. Gimber made a lasting impression on my life. Not because he was the pharmacist but because he showed genuine concern for me. He would always say "Michael one day you are going to do great things and if you'll work hard, you'll see it come to pass." I always believed that and still do today.

While going to school, I never considered myself as anyone special. I hung around with some of the "In Crowd" whatever that means, but I was also friends with a lot of people who you wouldn't consider the "In Crowd". I guess

I tried to fit into whomever's world I was a part of at the time. Because my main interest was definitely sports, my favorite teachers were always coaches. I had my heart set on being a professional athlete. At the age of ten, I had my picture taken in Chicago at a St. Louis Cardinals and Chicago Cubs ball game with Stan Musial, who told me that day that if I worked hard and used my natural talents that the Lord gave me, that one day I could stand on that same field as a player. In little league that same year, I managed to hit a grand slam and four home runs. Growing up I thought childhood would last forever and each day would be a series of home runs. Without a doubt, baseball was one of my favorite sports. In my freshman year I tried out for the Varsity team, and made it and played for four years. I thought I definitely must have been created for an athletic career somewhere. It was my life. And in all my dreams for the future I saw myself as a rising new star. How was I to know that these dreams would never be totally fulfilled, at least not in the way I had expected.

Several years had passed by when one day my dad asked me,

"Michael would you like to get in the car and ride with me to Michigan City and I'll let you go visit your friend Don?"

"Are you serious dad? Sure I'd love to go."

So there we were headed for Don's house, my childhood friend whom I hadn't seen in five or six years. He invited me to spend the weekend with him and go to church with him and his family on Sunday. At first I was hesitant about the Sunday event but I quickly realized I might as well. After all, it had been quite some time since I had last entered a church. My family were not Christians so it was never a very important issue in our lives. However, mom with her limited knowledge had often prayed with us when we were little. And, she tried to teach us the importance of believing in God.

Little did I know, when we entered the church that Sunday morning, that my life was beginning to take a drastic turn. The morning service was good, but it was the evening service that would have a profound effect on my life. That night the preacher got up to preach and announced that his message would be on "Hell". I thought to myself, that sounds like a good message for a preacher to preach. But I thought the girl sitting next to me was even better. Her name was Judy and I could tell I was falling in love. Of course time always goes by fast when you're having fun. Before I knew it the night was over and we were headed for home.

Over the next couple of weeks I thought a lot about the service and especially about Judy. Then out of the blue, Don called me and invited me to come for the weekend and go back to church with them. Getting a chance to see Judy again was worth the trip and any church service that I would have to sit through. Being a Christian wasn't something that I was yearning to do but I didn't mind just spending a few hours if it meant I could see Judy. That night the service went just like the previous one two weeks before. When it came time for the preacher to preach I was talking to Judy and the other young people who were sitting in the back row of the church and not really paying attention to the service.

I will never forget the next few moments, as long as I live. For it was during this period that the preacher got up and said, "I would like to preach to you on Hell Part II". I couldn't believe what I was hearing. Why didn't he preach that message last week while I was gone instead of saving it for me. Throughout the whole message he kept looking at me and when it was time for the message to end he gave an invitation. I remember bowing my head and closing my eyes just like everyone else. Yet when I closed my eyes I remember saying to myself, God why did he preach that message tonight? I can't go to the altar in front of all of these people. And after all, the preacher kept looking at me through the whole service. I bet everyone noticed him doing that. What I didn't know, was that my best friend was making a sneak attack on me. When I was saying to myself, "Lord, no way and not tonight" I suddenly felt a hand come down on my shoulder. I knew that at that moment no one else was beside me so I thought this must be the hand of God. I yelled out, "Yes Lord, I'm coming and I ran to the front!" Don's grandfather whom everyone called Grandpa stayed at the altar for quite some time praying with me. He quoted me two scriptures which have stuck with me all of my life.

II Corinthians 5:17 - Therefore if any man be in Christ, he is a new creature: old things are passed away; behold, all things have become new.

Psalm 30:5 - For His anger endureth but a moment; in His favor is life: weeping may endure for a night, but joy comes in the morning.

I found out later that it was my best friend's hand that was on my shoulder and I wanted to hit him. But, I was glad that on that night my life had taken a change for the better. It was January 21, 1967 and I had just become a Christian. I had asked Jesus to come into my life and take total control of me. I knew that my sins were forgiven and that I was on my way to Heaven. And only God knew the roads that I would travel on the way.

The next day, upon arrival at school I told my best friend Steve what had happened to me. We had been drinking buddies and always spent a lot of time together. When I told him I had just gotten saved, he looked at me in bewilderment and said, "What do you mean, were you in some kind of accident?" Being saved was as foreign to him as it had been to me before the previous night. But I knew that inside of me a change had taken place that just couldn't be denied. And now was my opportunity to tell others what Jesus had done in my life and that he could do it in their life as well. Not realizing it, this became my first opportunity to experience what being a minister was all about. Needless to say, disappointment came when Steve didn't get saved right there on the spot.

Anytime something great happens in your life you want people to know about it. When you're jumping up and down inside it's kind of hard to keep that from being noticed. That's the way I felt about my new relationship with Jesus. I had never felt so loved and so accepted in all of my life. And I wanted to tell the world. One day in the school library my friend Larry who was on the basketball team with me came in and sat down beside me. He said,

"Michael can we talk?" And I said,

"Sure Larry, What is it?"

As his head was bent down and his hands covered his mouth he began to tell me about all the remarks being made over my excitement of being saved.

"Michael, he said, I know everybody is giving you a hard time. They just don't understand and they keep thinking that in a couple of weeks you will get back to your normal self and give all this 'saved stuff ' up. But I've been watching you Michael and I want what you have."

There happened to be a little sound proof room off to the side of the library that I took Larry into so that we could continue talking in private. I shared my heart with Larry about how Jesus had so dramatically changed my life. Of course the Holy Spirit had already prepared Larry's heart, so I was able to quickly lead him to the Lord. Now there was at least two of us that we knew of that were on fire for Jesus at River Valley High School.

It's so easy to hide Jesus when you're in High School. People are afraid to take a stand. They are afraid of being laughed at. I guess I'll never understand that. It should be the other way around. Everyone that isn't saved should be the weirdo. Jesus gave His life for us and every good and perfect gift comes from Him. And yet half the time we are ashamed to admit his presence in our lives.

Joel 2:27 says, "And you shall know that I am in the midst of Israel and that I am the Lord your God, and none else; and my people shall never be ashamed.

As a Junior in High School it was important for me to stand up for the Lord. Within two weeks of getting saved it was time for elections in our youth group at church and I was elected the new youth leader. My best friend Don had been the youth leader but somehow was never able to cause the group to grow much. We started with 11 and with God's help, he used me to bring it to 144 in attendance. During that time the first 11 kids were striving to stay close to God and a couple of them ended up going into the ministry. During this time I had no idea that being a leader of a church youth group would some day lead me into the ministry. I never set out to be a preacher. In fact, if you would have told me that, I would have laughed at you and said there was no way. I wasn't about to give up a career of playing sports to be in the ministry. I thought the full time ministry was for those people who had nothing else that they were talented in. And me, well I had more talent and desire for sports than anything else that I could possibly imagine. I loved God with all of my heart. And, with my youthful mind, I thought a person would have to be crazy to choose to go into the ministry. Especially when I knew that would involve travel and pastoring a church of people who would never fully realize all the things that God could do for them. Anyway I had my whole life ahead of me and I was not in any hurry to spend it in Bible College or in the ministry. I was quite happy to just be involved in the church and to have all my many friends in the youth group.

By 1969 I had just begun singing in a quartet at church. There again I had no idea that the Lord wanted to use me in that capacity. To tell you the truth singing did not come easy for me. I had to develop my voice by many hours of practice. The first time I was invited to sing a solo at church I sang "The Old Rugged Cross" and I crucified it. I walked off of the platform with tears in my eyes and I said, "Lord I'm never going to sing again unless you do one of two things. Either change my voice or change the ears of the people who have to listen." Praise God he's done both over the years. I started off as a tenor and now I'm a baritone bass. And, this is just one example of how early in my walk with the Lord I found that He was always there willing to direct my life.

As a Christian, I have learned that there will be hard and difficult times that we must face. There will be times when it seems like no one really cares about the problems that you are facing. There will be times when you will have to stand alone because people will be afraid to stand with you. There will be times and situations when it seems like your prayers are bouncing off of Heaven and that no one, not even God, seems to care. But over and over again I've found out that God really does care. And that He is working all things out for your good if you love Him and follow after the plans and purposes that He has for your life.

I'm reminded of an incident that took place several years ago, while ministering in a city wide crusade. It involved a young man who had just turned 15 years of age. He was big for his age and when he went to school many of the kids would make fun of him. He even liked a very special girl in the school. But, she never had time for him and when he would come around she would make fun of him in front of her friends.

It was during the second week of the meeting, that he came with his family and before the service was over he walked to the front and accepted Jesus Christ as his Lord and Savior along with thirteen other young people. I remember his smile and the way he looked when he made that commitment that night and I remember talking to him for a few minutes afterwards. He told me how important it was for him to make that decision. I thought about it later that night and reminded myself of the words that my friend Debbie had spoken years earlier in the hospital, when she said, "Never forget what people look like when they first get saved, it's a beautiful sight to see."

It was during the sixth week of the meeting on a Friday night, that this 15 year old boy's mother came to the service alone and had an experience that left a mark on all of us. She had been caught up in the realm of the Spirit for over an hour when she got up and began to approach the pulpit where I was standing.

"Can I ask you a question?" she said softly.

"Sure" I said, not knowing what she was going to ask."

"I was just in the presence of the Lord and He was smiling when I first saw Him. But then as I approached Him, He suddenly began to cry and I thought I had done something wrong, but He spoke first."

"Everything is OK," he said. "I have everything in control." It was at that moment when He spoke those words that I suddenly realized that I was back in the service."

"What does it mean?" she said.

"I believe that He is letting you know that you are about to go through something very difficult in your life. But, He will be there with you and take control of the situation."

That evening when she arrived home, there was a note on the table from her son which stated that he had been going through some problems in his life. He said he didn't feel like anyone knew or understood what he was feeling except the Lord. And for some reason he wasn't even sure if the Lord was listening to him at the time. In his letter he told his parents that he was sorry for all of the problems that he had ever caused them and that he did not want to cause them any more grief. He closed with the fact that he loved them very much and that he hoped that they would forgive him for what he was about to do. And hopefully that the Lord would forgive him also. At first she thought that he had run away. So she ran to his bedroom only to find that his clothes and belongings were still there. Then she went into her bedroom and found him lying on the floor, with his father's gun in his hand and three letters that he had written to the Lord about his situation. He had shot himself in the head and had died about the same time that his mother had received her vision from the Lord.

Here was a young man that took his life, believing that no one cared and that no one understood his situation or problems. He had chosen to take the only way out that seemed possible for him. In his letters he tried to tell God how he felt. He said, "I know that you are real God, because I have experienced you more in the last two weeks than I ever have in my life. But, lately I have been going through depression and sorrow that I just can't seem to get over. I've been going through a lot of trials and situations in school as well as at home and it seems like nobody cares. I went to school and told everybody how excited I was about serving you. But they all laughed at me and made funny remarks. I'm 15 years old and I'm overweight and too big for myself. I just can't take the pressure, I feel like I'm on a dead end street." He drew a picture of an automobile and him being inside of it. You could see the speedometer and it was maxed out and there was a sign in the road directly in front of him that said, Dead End. In the second letter he talked about hearing voices all the time and having to deal with those voices that were telling him that he was no good and that he should end his life. He talked about going to his father and his father didn't really understand his problems. At the end of the letter he drew a picture of himself sitting up in an attic on top of an old chest. In front of him was a mirror and he was holding in his hand a sword that he had found in the chest. As he was looking in the mirror he saw death with the sword. And this represented the fact that all he could see and hear was that he was going to die because he just wasn't good enough. Death was speaking to him and the enemy was telling him lies. In the third letter, he asked for forgiveness. He tried to explain in the letters why he had done this terrible thing and he hoped that people wouldn't think badly of him for doing it. He just felt that he could no longer take the pressure that he was facing in life.

What he did not realize at the time, was that he was loved and that people did care. When the funeral took place many hundreds of people came including most of the school. As I read the letters that had been written to God about the kids and school, I noticed that everyone began to weep and cry. I asked people to pray with me the prayer of salvation and before the service was over almost every hand was raised as a testimony to this young man and the love that people had for him that day. What Satan had meant for evil, God turned it around for good.

> Life is full of memories
> The thoughts of every man
> Not always are they given
> Exactly as we'd planned.
>
> The ups and downs
> That life may bring
> Tend only to reveal
> An even fuller picture
> Of God's redeeming will.
>
> What's often seen as tragic
> God will work it for our good
> If we will just remember
> He said, "He always would."

Death where is your victory?
Oh Death, where is your sting?
We offer up before the Lord
This child we call a teen.

Teenagers are a blessing
That are given to reveal
The youth that's still in all of us
To recapture if we will.

So take a glimpse of the memories
With joy and not with pain
And remember with a tender heart
A love that still remains.

Copyright 1995 Victoria Lee

***

I have often wondered why people are so cruel to each other and why they feel the need to go along with the crowd. Why is it that we have to make fun of people and have such little regard for the feelings of others. It is not until the damage is done and we realize the outcome that we begin to cry and understand. If we'd stop and think, but for the grace of God, it could be any one of us in similar situations.

Each of you must face problems that at times seem overwhelming. You feel like there is no way out and that your tears could fill a huge vase. But, there is still a God in Heaven that is listening and waiting for you to "let go and let God."

Tomorrow is a new day and we cannot relive yesterday. But we can learn and go on in life knowing that in spite of the problems of today, there is a tomorrow. We can praise the Lord for the victory and know that "God's Answers are bigger than our Problems." He has the key to unlock all the chains that Satan and man may try to bind you with today.

Remember that "Joy comes in the Morning" in spite of how you feel today.

There is an old saying, "Today is the first day of the rest of your life!" and "Tomorrow is a brand new day."

***

"What time I am afraid,

I will trust in thee.

Psalm 56:3

"And they that know thy name

will put their trust in thee:

For thou, Lord, hast not forsaken

them that seek Thee.

Psalm 9:10

***

Chapter Three

A SHATTERED DREAM

It was May 1969, graduation from River Valley High School in Three Oaks, Michigan finally had arrived. Our school was made up of 900 students and those graduating were eager to pursue what life had to offer. It seemed as if the whole world was a fruit basket and we could pick from any variety of life that we so desired. Mine of course had still remained sports, sports and more sports. But, I also knew I had to further my education. I had wanted to go to the University of Indiana but because the basketball season was quickly approaching I decided to start out at the University of Indiana Extension in South Bend. So, there I was going to college in the daytime and playing basketball in the afternoon and evening. Then I would leave for work around 11 p.m. each night.

I was so excited about the future and how I was going to make my dreams come true. The industrial company that I worked for was located in Buchanon, Michigan. My job there was just a means of taking care of my financial needs. I had never intended to make a career out of it. Not me, I was on my way to a rewarding career that had excitement and elements of physical exertion. I had been working there for several weeks and they were training me as a swingman and operator for the large banjo transmissions. We made these transmissions that fit into heavy duty tractors and trailers. My job was working with the banjo machine. Before a transmission casing was molded on the inside and outside it was placed on a conveyor belt. The belt carried the transmission casing to the top of the machine where there was a furnace that heated it up to 1000's degrees Fahrenheit. Then the operator and swing man's job would be to push a button which in turn dropped the transmission casing. When it landed you would pick it up with tongs on each end and place it on the first mold which was the inside of the casing. After it would mold the inside you would take the tongs and flip it over and place it on the second mold. Then 6 foot clamps would come out of the machine and mold the outside. Those 6 foot clamps applied 2000 pounds worth of pressure to the transmission mold. The swingman would then pull the transmission casing out into some water and onto a conveyor belt that moved it on to next operation.

It was a snowy day on November 7, 1969. I had been to college and basketball practice earlier in the day. As I was getting ready to leave for work I noticed a little miniature Bible laying on my desk and I remember something inside of me said take it and I thought no I can't do that or they will make fun of me. I was only eighteen at the time and peer pressure still had a great deal of influence on me in spite of my longing desire to make a stand for God. But then I heard the voice again say, take it. I don't know how many of you have ever had a trial or argument with God that you fortunately lost, but I have. I took that little miniature Bible and hid it where no one could see it.

At 4:30 in the morning I came out of the room where we were having our lunch break at work and I remember going over and sitting behind one of the machines. I pulled out that little Bible and began to read the 23rd Psalm. The Lord is my Shepherd, and I read the 23rd, 24th and 25th Psalm. Then I came to the 26th Psalm and I read verses 1 through 3 just a few minutes prior to my accident. They read like this:

"Judge me, O Lord; for I have walked in mine integrity: I have trusted also in the Lord; therefore I shall not slide. Examine me, O Lord, and prove me; try my reins and my heart. For thy loving kindness is before mine eyes; and I have walked in thy truth."

I remember looking back at the second verse that said, "Examine me, O Lord." Just about that time the foreman came over and asked me and another friend to start up one of the machines that had not been used in several days.

As my friend went around to the back of the machine to turn on the power, I went around to the front. I was going to be the operator this particular day. I went over to the machine with an air gun and I began cleaning it out around the first mold area. Then I moved to the second mold where the big 6 foot clamps were. As I began to clean it out I heard the motors start up. Days before when the machine had last been in operation, it had been left in the midst of a cycle. As with a record player, when you reject it and pull the plug, the minute you plug it back in, it's going to complete it's cycle. Well this machine kicked back on right in the part of the cycle where the 6 foot clamps come back out. I was right in the middle of the clamps and standing very close. I was trying to get out when suddenly I could feel my leg being pulled into the machine. I desperately tried to turn to my right to find something to release the clamps but there was nothing there. As I turned back to my left, there in arms reach was a bright red button. I reached out and touched the button and it released the clamps immediately. I staggered forward and hit my head on a steel girder. Then staggered back and fell off of a 2 foot platform onto a concrete floor landing on the back of my head. In both cases, I should have been knocked unconscious. But the Lord kept me awake.

The pain was so unbearable that I thought at any moment that I would lose consciousness. I could feel my leg throbbing and I knew that something terrible had just happened. But, my mind was racing so fast with the events taking place, that I was having a hard time trying to fully realize the scope of what had just occurred. After laying on the ground for what seemed like the longest time, I was able to raise my head and look down at the leg that had been crushed a few minutes earlier. My leg was twisted and I could see the thigh bone sticking out on both sides of where my pants had been moments before. I could see that my knee was shattered as the blood began to flow out of my leg and onto the ground. I saw that my leg from the knee down, was bent in a right angle. No one knew what had happened not even the foreman or the young man that had been working with me.

It was later during the trial that I shared in court what had happened. I was shown pictures by the opposing lawyers which stated that there was no red button in arms length and there was no way that I could have reached out and touched it. They also said there were three red buttons on the opposite wall from where I was being pulled into the machine, but there was no way that I could have touched them either. But they could not dispute the fact that something had to release the clamps, otherwise I would not be here today. My leg would have been crushed smaller than my hand and I would have died from the loss of blood. I thank God, that He knows how to put the right things in the right place at the right time.

Laying on the floor and looking down at the leg that had been crushed, I began to cry out and suddenly people began to rush out of the break room. My friend rushed over to where I was laying on the ground and knelt down beside me. Within a few moments, four men placed me on a stretcher and ran me the length of the building where they waited for the ambulance to come. While they waited, those four men did something that I will never forget. They got on their knees and began to pray. I don't know if they were Christians or not, but I'm glad that someone taught them the importance of praying. People began rushing up from all over the factory. The foreman asked me if there was anything that I needed. All I could think of was the small Bible in the pocket of my jacket. Within seconds, he pulled back the covers that were covering me and handed me the Bible which I clasped over my heart. His next words will forever remain vivid in my mind. He said,

"If you have the guts to bring this thing with you to work, then have the guts to believe that He will take care of you!"

Within minutes, I was rushed to the hospital where I was taken into the emergency room. Doctors and nurses were frantically tending to my needs and trying to keep me alive.

I remember looking up at the clock on the wall and it was almost 5 o'clock in the morning. Suddenly a nurse came into the room and spoke to the doctor and said, "We don't have enough blood of his type to get him to the medical center in Ann Arbor, Michigan." A few moments later, the phone rang and on the other end was an artery specialist who was scheduled to fly to the west coast in a couple of hours and she wanted to know if there was anyone there that needed her help. Also on duty at the time, was Dr. Leslie Bodnar, one of the top orthopedic doctors in the nation. I learned a long time ago, that nothing is coincidence with

God. He also knows how to put the right people in the right place at the right time.

The damage from the compression of the clamps had crushed my leg severely. For many hours the medical people worked and operated on me trying to rebuild it. Following the operation, I was placed in a room and for almost three days, I was in a coma. During this time after a blood clot developed at the base of my foot gangrene set in. Therefore, they again prepared me for more surgery. It was during this time that I woke up from the coma I had been in and after looking down at the leg that had been crushed, I looked out into the hallway and saw it filled with people. My mother and dad and sisters and brother-in-laws, members of the church and the pastor were all talking amongst themselves.

Suddenly I saw Mom bury her head into dad's shoulder as the doctor began speaking to them and then I saw them crying. I thought to myself, "Lord why are they crying, when everything is OK?" "My leg is alright, it's just broken and in no time I will be out playing ball again." It was at that moment that I heard that still small voice of the Lord speaking to me. "The doctor has just told them that you will have to have your leg removed or you will die. I want you to smile like your parents smiled when they came to the hospital days earlier and wanted to be strong for you."

It amazes me sometimes how skeptical people can be when you tell them that the Lord talks to you. It merely shows that we don't know the Lord in the way we should and we don't understand His ways. Even those who claim to know Him have a hard time believing that God speaks to people today. Yet the Book of Psalms tells us, "Be still and know that I am God." Psalm 46:10

Within moments the doctor came back into the room and noticed that I had come out of the coma. My family began to stand around the bed and the doctor began asking me questions and trying to tell me that everything was going to be alright. I tried to speak but nothing happened. When I tried again, the doctor put his head down next to my lips, trying to hear my voice and I asked him just one question in a whisper, "How Much?"

Suddenly he pulled his head back and I looked into his eyes and I noticed a tear as he spoke. He said, "How did you know? We were not going to tell you for fear that it might hurt your chances and cause you to go into shock and withdraw." I looked at him and whispered the only thing that I knew he might understand at the moment and that was "Jesus".

One of the most difficult things in the world was waking up a day later and looking down at the sheets that were covering me and seeing only a lump of bandages where a part of me used to be. Gone was the career that I had planned all of my life. Gone were the dreams and hopes that I had of one day playing major league baseball and being someone special and important.

For over two months, I laid in a hospital bed as my robust 185 pound body declined into a weakened, frail, pitiful young man. I had a body cast on from my chest down and could not move except with the help of other people. The major holidays came and went and still nothing seemed to change. In fact, it was during this time, that I became very bitter inside and decided that I must have done something wrong in my life, that would cause God to allow this to happen to me.

Finally one night just before Christmas, I was laying in my room at two o'clock in the morning when suddenly a doctor appeared in the room. Having not expected anyone, I was shocked when suddenly the person began to laugh and I looked into the eyes and face of one of my best buddies, who had traveled over an hour to come and tell me what the Lord had spoken to him earlier that evening. Yet in order to get into the hospital, he had to sneak in and find some clothing to get past the nurses. I will never forget his words as he spoke,

"Michael, the Lord told me to tell you, that It's Not The End, But Just The Beginning!"

How many times have your dreams and visions been shattered by disappointments and failures or by friends and loved ones who couldn't understand your desire to get ahead and do something different with your life? How many times, instead of encouragement, they have made fun of you, with their belief that you would never amount to anything in life.

All over America right now, people are making the biggest decisions of their lives. They are making decisions that will not only affect them personally, but also affect their spouses and their family and friends. Right now, there are some of you reading this book that are about to make the biggest decision of your life, but you are unsure because no one seems to care. And if they do, you're afraid to involve them in your decision for fear that you might be ridiculed or fail once again.

Many people are afraid to make important decisions and are afraid of "rocking or stepping out of the boat" because they are too concerned about what other people might think. Also, many are afraid that they might not succeed where others have already failed. However, we live in one of the greatest nations on the face of the earth, a country where each of us has the chance to succeed in life or just be one of the crowd. Opportunities knock each day and yet many people will not open their door to success, for fear of what it might cost them. They also might fear that they will not acquire what they are setting their goals for in this life.

The story of Joseph in the Bible, is one of the greatest success stories of someone who "dared to dream", even when others told him that it could never be done. Yet his dream did not come to pass right away without first experiencing many failures along the way. Here was a person that had to experience the rejection of family and friends and then face death and finally be sold into captivity. While in captivity and after many years of giving his best to his employers, he was accused of a crime that he did not commit and thrown into prison. Joseph stayed in prison until God finally vindicated him and made him the Prime Minister of a great nation.

My dreams were shattered and my heart was broken for the moment, but I still had a hope that the world and the enemy could not take away and like Joseph, I was prepared to dream another dream. Maybe you have never had to experience what Joseph went through. But, you probably have faced similar situations in your own life that left you discouraged and fearful and wanting to just quit and give up on everyone and everything in life.

Maybe you're facing your own "SHATTERED DREAMS AND BROKEN HEARTS" and you're wondering if those dreams will ever come true. You will never know until you try. Your gifts and abilities were given to you for a purpose in life and until you decide that it is worth trying and working and giving everything you have for it, you will never know the meaning of true success.

While in the hospital one day, I was visited by a couple that I never knew and have never seen again. But, they were real and they shared with me the meaning of being an "over comer" in life. They were married and they had been in an accident which cost both of them their legs. However, now they were traveling all over America on their motorcycles with their new artificial legs and sharing the hope and dreams that they had discovered through knowing Jesus Christ as their Lord and Savior. They gave me a book titled, "Reach For The Sky", about a top fighter pilot during World War II that flew for Britain even with an artificial leg. He never gave up and he never quit even when things seemed like they were impossible to accomplish.

Maybe you're there right now and it seems like everything is falling apart and that no one seems to care! I know, because I have been there myself and yet I learned through those most difficult times that I was never alone. I learned that I had a friend that was closer than any brother or sister. And this friend was someone that would never desert me or make fun of my plans or dreams. He was someone who cared about me and about what I thought and felt. Someone who didn't tell me, that it couldn't be done and someone who laughed with me and not at me and someone who even cried with me, when I was hurting. He was someone who wrapped His arms around me and told me that it was alright to fail because I wasn't a failure and that I was learning how to be victorious. I knew that He still loved me, in spite of my insecurities and sins and problems. And, He wanted me just the way I was, so that He could show me how to improve my life, by trusting in Him.

Eventually when the days grew into weeks, I found myself needing to fill some of my waking hours with some soothing music. So, I began to play my guitar and sing every night after visiting hours. I was on a floor in the hospital that was normally reserved for elderly people. Every night I would yell out from my room, "Who wants to hear a song?" You could hear people yelling out from their rooms the songs they wanted to hear. And then one night a little lady across the hall from me said,

"Michael would you sing "In the Garden?"

So I began to sing and usually when I would finish she would say, "Thank You Michael, Good Night." But this time she didn't say anything. I waited and waited and then finally I said to another lady across the hall that I guess she had gone to sleep and she said, "I don't know, let me check, maybe there is something wrong." Then we rang for the nurses and the next thing I knew Code Blue was on and she obviously had passed away during the song. Life is so short, we need to live it to it's fullest.

James 4:14 says, "Whereas you know not what shall be on the morrow. For what is your life? It is even a vapor, that appeareth for a little while and then vanisheth away."

I realized then that I had ministered to her but it was time for her to go be with the Lord. Even at age eighteen, with part of one leg missing and laying in a hospital bed God was still trying to show me that He had a call on my life.

***

"For the gifts and calling of God are without repentance."

Romans 11:29

"And Samuel said unto Jesse, are here all thy children? And he said, there remaineth yet the youngest, and, behold, he keepeth the sheep. And Samuel said unto Jesse, send forth and fetch him; for we will not sit down til he comes forth. And he sent, and brought him in.

Now he was ruddy, and he was withal of a beautiful countenance, and goodly to look at and the Lord said, arise and anoint him: for this is he. Then Samuel took the horn of oil, and anointed him in the midst of his brethren: and the Spirit of the Lord, came upon David from that day forward.

1 Samuel 16:11-13
***

Chapter Four

THE ANOINTING AND THE CALLING

In January of 1970, after being in the hospital for two and a half months I was released and headed for home. Mom and dad had so lovingly prepared my room for my expectant return. Everyone was trying to do everything they could to make me feel comfortable. Of course I was on crutches and in a wheelchair most of the time. When I had left for work two and a half months earlier, I had two strong legs that could run like lightning. But now even with the aid of crutches, I could hardly move across the living room floor. It wasn't easy coming home that day and realizing that I would never again walk around these rooms like I once had.

After about six months, Mom and dad wanted to do something special for me so they decided we'd take a little trip. It was a nice diversion for a while. We visited several places and saw a lot of things. Except for the occasional extra effort it took to transport me from one location to the other, it helped to get my mind temporarily off of my condition. When we arrived back home, I decided it was time to go back to church and get involved the best way I could. Of course, everyone invited me back with wide open arms. The love that they showed toward me was a tremendous way to help me begin to re-adjust to what had once been very familiar surroundings.

To my surprise, two ladies came up to me and shared an enlightening, yet unknown episode to the previous events of my life. They said that prior to the accident one of them that week and the other one the day before had felt impressed to pray for me but their schedules were so busy that they didn't do it. They felt that if they had intervened and prayed like the Holy Spirit was urging them to do, that it may have made a change in the events that took place.

It is so important for us to listen to what God is telling us in our hearts to do. If He brings some ones name to you, He expects you to pray and intercede for them. Because they are about to go through something. We can't be too busy to pray, we must be willing to be used. We are His hands extended. We are the eyes that He sees through. When someone needs a helping hand, that hand just might be you.

Have you ever wondered why God would call you? Maybe it was because of those special talents that you have that you have hidden all of your life. Maybe it's that strong voice that He has blessed you with or the ability to play an instrument or two. Maybe it was because of your writing ability or the gift of speaking to a crowd in such a way that you captivated them. Maybe it was your strong sense of hospitality or your warm touch that put everyone at ease. Or maybe it was your strong testimony of how God has changed your life. Have you asked Him to allow you to share about it all over America? Yet you still have a hard time sharing on your job or in the school or maybe sometimes even in your church. Well, everyone of us have been placed on this earth for a purpose. We are not a mistake. All of us have a part to play and a role to fit into. But, sometimes we are not willing to make the strong commitment to see our planned purpose come to pass. It's hard to understand the ways of the Lord unless you spend enough time with Him. Even then, His ways remain far above our ways. It's hard for us to believe that God would actually want to use us for so many worthwhile things. But God never created anyone that wasn't important. Your very talents are exactly what He needs to fulfill His plan on this earth. All He wants you to do is acknowledge your talents and be bold enough to harness them. You might say, "What if I don't know what they are?" Then begin looking at the things that you are the best at and that bring you the most joy. Most likely they are linked to exactly what God has planned for you. The Bible say, "Seek ye first the kingdom of God and His righteousness and all these things will be added unto you."

Sometimes we wonder why would God want to use someone that has made so many mistakes. And we may ask, how could God love me when I've shown such a lack of commitment and responsibility when it comes to the things of the Lord? But you see, God is always patient and understanding. And, He wants you to fulfill your role in life even more than you do.

We have all thought at one time or the other, why would God want to use me when He has so many other people to choose from. We want to trust Him and frequently want him to bless us in life, as long as we don't have to make major moves or shake ups in the safety zones that we have built up for ourselves and our families. Doesn't the Bible say that God uses the foolish things of the world to confound the wise? If we are presently experiencing hard times and He has to use us right now, it might seem odd and down right strange. Surely He knows that this is a bad time in our lives and maybe another day would be better. However, it could be He knows something that we don't because many of the things of God are still way beyond our comprehension.

I am often reminded of the story that has been told about a nineteenth-century Sunday School teacher who had a chance to lead a shoe clerk to Christ. This young man was from Boston at the time and his name was Billy Sunday. The man Kimball, who led him to Christ was no one special and was not considered a big name in the ministry, yet he loved God and God knew his name.

Soon after finding Christ, this shoe salesman became an evangelist. And, then Billy, the evangelist influenced many people's lives, including a man by the name of Fredrick Meyer. This young preacher started ministering on many college campuses across the country and while giving an invitation one day, he led another young man by the name of J. Wilbur Chapman to the Lord. It wasn't long after, that this young man became involved in the work of the YMCA and made arrangements for a baseball player to come to town and share the gospel of Jesus Christ. The revival went so well, that many in the town wanted the Christian leaders to have another revival and they invited a great preacher by the name of Mordecai Hamm to preach in Charlotte, North Carolina. The meeting was scheduled to end a week earlier, but many asked if it could go on for one more week, and during that week a young man by the name of Billy Graham came to know Jesus Christ as his personal Savior.

It is unlikely that any of these preachers could have been able to see that far ahead in their ministry or in their lives. It would have been hard to foresee the impact that they would have on other people and on those that would come to know Christ as their Lord and Savior. However, their limited view of the future, did not keep them from their calling or destination. Maybe we need to be reminded sometimes of the one who is doing the calling and discover that He truly knows where we are at and what we are going through in our lives. Nothing is impossible with God.

There comes a time in each of our lives when we must answer the call of God. Laying in a hospital bed for almost three months, gave me plenty of opportunity to think about what I would do with my life once I had been released. I often thought about the words, that my friend had shared that night when he came to the hospital with the message that the Lord had given him for me. I could not help but think and dwell on those words, over and over again, "It's Not The End, But It's Just The Beginning."

How simple and easy those words seemed to take control of my thoughts. It was as though God was trying to tell me that He had everything under control. Yet, why was I still feeling like the most important things in my life were being taken from me? It was a constant battle not to become bitter and angry with God. I found it was easy to place guilt on someone that I could not see and yet I knew that He was still real in my life. I wanted to cry out "Why Me Lord?" Why not someone who deserved it or someone that was cruel and mean? I kept fighting the feelings deep inside that kept coming day after day in which I was trying to figure God out and figure out why He would allow these things to happen to me. It was a difficult time in my life and there was no where to run and no place to hide. No one seemed to be able to understand the feelings that were going on inside of my head. Not even my preacher or the doctor could answer all the questions that kept repeating themselves over and over in my mind. The answer could only come from two places. The Lord and those who had gone through similar experiences.

During these trying times, the church filled a lot of the gap that was missing. Thankfully my preacher, Reverend Yake spent time trying to encourage me and telling me that God had a very special purpose for my life. He said I needed to wait in His presence and seek His direction. Those seem like such easy words to say. But, in reality they are the most crucial and significant words of advice that anyone can receive. ONLY GOD knows the answers for your life. Yet most of us run around asking everybody under the sun what they think we're supposed to be doing, instead of asking God what He wants us to do. Do we really want the quick - fix answers, those microwave-2 second solutions to the most important things in our lives? Or, shouldn't we be willing to sit before the feet of Jesus until He makes His will known to us? Shouldn't "That I might know Him, and the power of His resurrection," be the cry of each one of our hearts?

One night at church when I was feeling so lost and yearning for some answers, one of the dearest men I ever knew came to the altar where I was praying. It was everyone's favorite "Grandpa", the one who had prayed with me for so long the night I first accepted the Lord in my life. I respected and admired him so much as a Godly man and I was always eager to hear what he had to say. As he knelt down and wrapped his arms around me to pray, he said,

"Michael, I believe God has allowed this to happen to you because He is calling you and preparing you for the ministry. I believe that

God is going to use you to reach a lot of hurting people."

I remember looking at him with tears in my eyes and saying,

"Do you really believe that?" "Yes I do!" he said. "Your work with the youth group and your desire to sing has prepared you for the work that He wants you to do in life."

We may never understand the ways of the Lord. But if there is one thing that I do know, it is that His hand is upon your life and now it's up to you to decide whether or not you will answer His call. It will not be easy and there will be times when you will want to quit and give up. There will be times when the enemy will try to destroy you, but don't quit and don't allow the enemy to get the victory by defeating you with problems or discouragement's that you cannot overcome in life."

So many people give up when they are right on the brink of their miracle. All of us are not called to be preachers, but all of us are called. The question is, do you want to do your own thing or do you want to do what God's thing is for you? Or in other words, why not choose the "First Best" instead of what may be the "Second Best".

Leaving the altar that night, I made up my mind that "yes" God had called me and that "yes" I would respond to His calling and His anointing in my life. That night the preacher and grandpa had laid hands on me and asked the Lord to anoint me for the calling and the special work that He wanted me to do.

Arriving home that night, I had decided to tell my family that it was time to make a change and that I had decided to go into the ministry. Yet when I shared this great news with my dad, he looked at me with strong disappointment. He said he had hoped that I would work at the same factory that his father and him had worked at for many years. There was a shouting match and even a few choice words that my dad used to express his anger and disappointment with me. Here I was full of encouragement and excitement about the purpose I thought God had for my life and within minutes I found myself on a discouraging battlefield. Through it all, mom never said a word until I went into my room and then she came in and told me she loved me and hoped that I would take time to think about it some more. But, I had made up my mind and decided that night, that in time, I would serve the Lord and be a part of the ministry. The presence of The Holy Spirit speaking to me that night had been so real, that it would be impossible for me to do anything else with my life.

***

"Said I not unto thee,

that if thou wouldest believe,

thou shouldest see the glory of God?"

John 11:40

"But without Faith it is impossible

to please Him;

For he that cometh to God

must believe that He is,

and that He is a rewarder

of them that diligently seek Him.

Hebrews 11:6

***

Chapter Five

ALL THINGS ARE POSSIBLE, IF YOU ONLY BELIEVE

In the fall of 1970 I started attending Eastern Michigan University in Ypsilanti, Michigan. I thought I would attend there for a couple of years and then transfer to a Bible College for any further training that I might need in the future. That fall, two things would happen that would delay my going into the ministry and would have a profound affect on my life and would help me years later for the calling that God had placed in me.

The first was the forming of my new singing group, "The New Generation Singers", a group of young people from the campus that was made up of all denominations. Music had been a part of my life ever since I was a child listening to my mother sing. I used to spend hours listening to records and singing along with them. I would always learn the parts and pretend that one day I would sing before thousands of people in concert and on television. During the previous couple of years I had sung in the church choir and had formed a quartet in the church. When I graduated and attended the local university, I had attended another church and formed another quartet. We had been scheduled to sing in a quartet concert with many other groups just before my accident. In fact, just after the accident, there was a night that I will never forget. It was the night of a southern gospel concert in our hometown in which my quartet was to sing and while laying in my bed thinking about not being able to be there, I heard a knock on the door at about 8:30 p.m. When I said, "Come In", I just about fell out of bed. I saw some of the greatest people in Gospel music come through the door and led by a dear friend, Lauren Matthews.

There was J.D. Sumner, Buck and Dottie Rambo, The Lefveres, Mom and Pop Speer, James Blackwood and The Happy Goodmans. Some of the best musicians and singers that I had ever had the chance to hear and now they were in my room at the hospital asking if they could pray for me and telling me that they wished I could be there that night in the concert. Music was now becoming a big part of my life and yet I had never taken a lesson and did not know how to read music. But, I knew that one day the Lord would give me a voice that would be anointed so that I could minister to people. So now, my job was to keep working and practicing until I had the confidence to know that it was not just me doing it but that God had a plan. He wanted me to reach others and be a blessing for the Lord.

The second thing that would change my life, was the day that the doctor called from back home and told me that he had something that he wanted to tell me. It was time to be fitted with a new leg after all this time. Just the thought of walking made me cry and I began to thank God for the chance to once again be able to. Sometimes we all seem to take for granted those things that God has blessed us with in life. We should be thankful each day for those blessings and realize that there are others who do not have the same blessings.

I remember going to the doctor's office with my mother. While she waited in the reception area I went into the other room with fear, nervousness and apprehension. "What if I can't walk with it, Lord?", I thought! Sitting down in the chair I waited for the doctor to enter the room. I can't tell you the joy and the excitement that was building up in me as he walked in with an artificial leg under his arm. No words could be spoken to express my thoughts and feelings, except that I was going to walk again for the first time in almost two years.

"There are two things that I have to tell you Michael."

"I don't care doc", I said in my excitement. "All that I know, is that I'm going to walk right out of here as soon as you put this leg on me."

"You don't understand, Michael, it won't be that easy!"

"Yes it will doc, just hurry and put it on!"

"Are you sure?", he said looking at me as if I was crazy.

"Yes, I am, I'm going to walk for you and mom and God."

He came over to where I was sitting and began to strap the leg on and told me to take my time and use the parallel bars that were in front of me. Yet all that I could think of was walking right out of that room and back to school and never looking back. What took place next, changed my life and my thinking for a long time to come. As I stood up to take those first steps, I fell flat on my face. I was so embarrassed as the doctor came over and picked me up and placed me back in the chair. Later I realized that it wouldn't be the last time that I would fall but like the hands of the doctor, the hands of God would pick me up when I fell as a Christian and set me back on the Rock that I had fallen off of in life.

"Are you ready to listen now?", he asked.

I nodded and he began to share with me two things.

"First Michael you will have to learn how to walk again just like a baby has to learn. Your sense of balance is gone and it will take time to learn those simple things that you used to take for granted. Second, you will have to realize that because of the damage to your leg and the loss of most of the femur bone which lies directly above your knee, you will not be able to walk very well and if you do, it will be with a limp for the rest of your life. But that won't matter because most people with artificial legs walk with a limp. Also any participation on your part in sports can only be done in a non professional basis."

I had grown to care about that doctor as a friend as well as a physician, but sometimes he could make me angry and this was one of those times. I didn't want to believe what he was telling me because I was convinced that "nothing was impossible with God." Leaving the doctor's office that afternoon, I was determined that nothing was going to stop me from accomplishing things that were important to me in life. The drive back home would have been longer, except mom always seemed to know what to say at the right time.

"What do you think?" she said.

"I think he's wrong! I responded.

"What are you going to do about it?",
she smiled.

"I don't know yet, but I'll think
of something."

"Whatever you do, don't be foolish, because the doctors know what they are talking about", she said.

"I know that mom, but they are not me and I believe the Lord will help me, if I give Him the chance."

For the rest of the trip, I knew that mom cared and it hurt her to know that I was being disappointed again. Yet she didn't have to always say something, for me to know that she cared and understood how I felt about things. It was as if she could read my mind and knew that I would probably do something anyway, in spite of what the doctors or anyone else might say about it. It was just her way of saying, "Don't do anything that you might regret later." She knew that I had always taken chances in life and that if anyone could over come this situation, it would be me.

That night arriving back at campus, I went into my room and with the door closed and no one else around, I sat down on the bed and prayed. Then I strapped the leg on and stood to my feet. I must have stood there for the longest time, waiting and wondering if I would once again fall down. But this time nothing happened. Instead I took a couple of steps and stopped and turned around and walked back to the bed and thought to myself, "Lord you said, everything that is impossible with man is possible with God."

Two nights later, my singing group was ministering on a Sunday night at a church in Ann Arbor, Michigan just a few miles from the school. The host pastor was Dr. Harold Evans. They had been advertising for weeks that we were going to be there, ministering in music and the Word of God. The auditorium was packed with over five hundred people.

I had already made up my mind to wear the artificial leg that night. It was the first time that any member of the group or anyone in the audience had ever seen me with two legs. Even my best friend Tim Previtt was concerned that I might fall or be hurt in some way. But, I had assured him that everything was going to be alright and that the Lord would take care of me that night.

Half way through the service the pastor stopped the program to pray for a lady who was dying in the hospital. Then they began to sing a chorus, that became the theme song for our ministry through the years. "Only Believe, That All Things Are Possible, When You Only Believe."

I was standing to the left of the pulpit, when suddenly I heard a voice speaking and it said, "Sit down your crutches and walk." I opened my eyes, but there was no one there. I thought I was going crazy, when suddenly I heard the voice again say, "Sit down your crutches and walk." "Lord if that is you", I thought to myself, "then you saw what happened in the doctor's office. I'm not going to fall down in front of all of these people" and "devil if that's you, then you're crazy anyway and I'm not going to do it!" The words were so clear in my head and suddenly the voice came again, "What are they singing? Then believe and walk!"

At that moment, the pastor had finished singing the song and turned the service back to me. As the group started to get back into formation on the platform, I remember sitting down my crutches as the music was still playing. Without looking at anyone, I started walking across the platform until I reached the pulpit. I had taken over fifteen steps and when I looked up, everyone was crying, because what the doctor said would take years, the Lord was able to do in a moment of time. God had performed a miracle that night in front of over five hundred people, including my two sisters whom I didn't even know were there. All of a sudden one of them walked up to the altar and accepted the Lord as her Savior.

From that moment on, there were no longer any doubts or fears about the calling of the Lord on my life. There would no longer be any questions as to whether or not God was alive or real. In spite of my hurts and pains and in spite of all my problems, He had reached down His hand of mercy on me that night and showed me that He still cared and that He was still in control.

Growing up as children, we were taught or given the impression that maybe things would last forever. This included marriages and jobs and relationships. Yet now we live in a generation that destroys that myth in many ways. Maybe one of the most disturbing things about all of this, is how quickly these things have changed and come to pass during the past thirty or forty years. Too many people have forgotten the morals and values that once made our nation so great.

Spending time in the hospital and then watching the Lord perform the miracles for me during those next two years, showed me just how important life really was. It also reminded me that we should live each day to the fullest, never taking for granted the many things that we have been blessed with.

The Bible states in James 4:14 - "For we know not of tomorrow, for what is our life but a vapor that appeareth for a little while and then vanishes away."

Walking across that platform and then down three stairs that night, showed me just how important each of us are to a living God. It would have been easy to have experienced another defeat, by falling down that night. But the Lord showed me that He was in control of my life and in every situation that I would have to face in the future.

Once you have been called and chosen, then there is no turning back. In spite of the difficulties and in spite of the hardships and even in spite of what anyone else has to say about you, the Bible says, "God's gifts and callings are without repentance." So in other words, there is nothing that you could do that would change God's mind about what He wants you to accomplish in life. The only thing that can keep it from happening is your refusal to believe it and persevere until it comes to pass. As a preacher or Christian, you may sin and make mistakes in life, but you will never lose your calling. You may fail God and man, but you will always be God's anointed and chosen one for your created purpose. I have a saying that I really believe for this generation of time, especially when the big name ministries began to fall. Too many people have been passing judgement and making statements that should have never been made. They are saying these things to the world, in the pulpits or behind closed doors.

Well, I believe, only God can put them in and only God can take them out! David did not stop being king when he sinned and committed murder and adultery and preachers don't stop being preachers just because they make mistakes. The prophet Nathan said it best when the people of Israel wanted to stone David and Bathsheba. "Touch Not God's Anointed." Because God never takes back His promises.

The life of Christ was one of going where the sinners were and touching them in the midst of their infirmities. Not one of being so separate that people can not reach you. Maybe it's the training or the fear of getting too close to people that causes preachers to keep their distance from the people that they are trying to minister to each day. I do not believe that God ordained for his ministers to have unlisted numbers. Or to run off of the platform after they've preached their message and out the door so that people can't talk to them and ask questions. We sometimes leave the impression that we don't want to be bothered by petty talk or annoyed by people who want to take up our time. There may be times of exceptions in this area. One of them is when the ministry is walking under the anointing of the Holy Spirit and total attention needs to be focused on hearing from Him. However most of the time we need to be more genuine in our concern and more active in our involvement.

After that remarkable night in church I spent the next six months in therapy at the University of Michigan in Ann Arbor. The doctor had told me I should take at least a year of therapy but I was able to do remarkably well in half the time. I learned very quickly to walk with my new leg and in fact I even started learning to run. Of course, there were those moments in which I forgot that I had an artificial leg and tried to do the same things that I had done before the accident. Sometimes, those turned into embarrassing exploits.

For instance, there was the baseball game that I was participating in back home four months after learning how to walk with my new leg. I had come to bat in the sixth inning and there were two men on base at the time. The player before me had dug the plate out trying to get into a good stance. The only problem was that he forgot to replace the dirt in the hole that he had made. Of course when I came up to bat, I had forgotten to check the home plate area. All I could think of at the time was getting a hit and driving in the winning runs.

What happened next, was a little blurry for a long time. You see I got a base hit and when I began to run, my foot caught the home plate area and I immediately stumbled and fell down. When I hit the ground I was knocked out. Also, the pressure of my fall caused me to tumble forward, thus bending the artificial foot backwards to the point of breaking. Everyone was watching and the crowd began to scream. The ankle part of the leg snapped and the foot went flying high into the air and landed about ten feet from where I had fallen. There was immediate pandemonium and several people began to go into shock. The pitcher kept saying over and over again as they took him off of the field, "There's no blood, how can someone's foot fall off and there not be any blood?"

One woman cried out, "I hope that's not real," and then she fainted. The center fielder who was chasing my hit, caught the ball on the ground and picked it up to throw it into the infield. When he saw me fall and saw the foot go into the air, he dropped the ball and forgot to throw it in which allowed two runs to score and we won the game. I might also note, that the umpires did not know how to rule on this one, because there was nothing in the rule book to tell them what to do when a players' foot flies off in the middle of a game.

Life is full of uncertainties and things which happen that we do not plan. Yet we must learn how to overcome those problems and obstacles when faced with situations that may come each day. Losing a leg twice taught me that you are never really ready to face tomorrow's problems, unless you have adequate assurance today about your own life. The only way to have that assurance is through Jesus Christ. Oh you can say you have assurance even if you don't have Jesus in your life, but you're only kidding yourself. Don't we always call on Him when something bad happens in our lives? Well, then having a relationship with God should add to our assurance that even in the midst of the trial, He has everything in control. Also, when we don't really know Him and only know about Him, then we're never really sure if He's hearing our cry for help.

Two months later following my baseball accident and being fitted with a new leg, I once again went back to college with an earnest expectation for the future. Arriving back at school, I began thinking about the future and what tomorrow might bring in my life.

One day as I was sitting in the college courtyard where the guys were practicing baseball, I saw a couple of the guys that I had played against in high school. Sitting there, I thought about the career that I had lost in basketball and in baseball because of the accident. The thought of participating in another baseball game hadn't even been on my mind, especially since I had broken one artificial leg already. But I remember thinking, I could have been one of them. Then the Lord began to speak to me and said, "Remember it's been done before." Two nights earlier the story of Monty Stratton had been on television. He was with the Chicago White Soxs in 1927 when he had his leg shot off in a hunting accident. He thought his career was over but he made a come back. He was the first professional player to ever play professional baseball with an artificial leg. He played from 1927 to 1941. I suddenly realized, what I wanted to do with my life, before I entered the full time preaching ministry. I wanted to make a come back into a sport that I had dreamed would be my lifetime career. And I said, "If he can, I can."

Those were some difficult times in my life. I had to look inside of myself and see what I really wanted to happen to me. I had to ask myself, "How important is it for me to play sports again?" Soon, I had the opportunity to give it my best shot. I've always been one that had to show and prove to everyone that I could do things that other people thought could not be done. In order to be picked for the baseball team I had to make it through four cuts, which I did. But, when I went to the athletic board to see if my name was on the list, it wasn't. I was so hurt and angry that I didn't know what to do. I had always been such a good athlete when I had two good legs and to be truthful, I was pretty proud of myself with an artificial leg as well. But, for some reason I wasn't picked to be on the team.

I drove into Detroit that night just to get away for a while and lick my wounds, so to speak. This was another setback and another loss in my life and yet I could not and would not believe that it was happening to me all over again. I had worked harder than anyone and I had told the coach that I didn't want any publicity, I just wanted to show him that I could still play baseball in spite of my handicap. For the next four hours, I walked the streets of Detroit just full of anger. I was hoping that someone would pick a fight with me just so I could beat them up.

When I arrived back at the dorm in the wee hours of the morning, some of the guys were waiting for me. They said, "Coach wants to see you in the morning." But I said, "I don't want to see him." Reluctantly though I went to his office later on in the morning. He began to share with me how much flack he had gotten over his decision to keep me off of the team. His wife, his secretary and a lot of the players were all upset with his decision. They all knew how much the team meant to me and how very hard I had worked to be on it. I had even raised the most money during our fund raiser and they therefore awarded me a new baseball mitt and bat. Coach O'Strike looked at me and said,

"Michael I cut you for the wrong reasons. Therefore, I'm going to make sure that you play on the team because you are a good player in spite of your handicap.

"Alright," I yelled, trying not to get too excited as I left the room amidst the joy and excitement of the whole office staff. I had made it and yet I knew that the work that had been put into getting this far, was nothing compared to what would be expected of me in the future.

So, I made the team in my freshman year at Eastern Michigan University. What a joy and thrill that was. I was excited and thankful at the same time. Coach O'Strike one of the winningest coaches in NCAA baseball had given me one of the greatest opportunities that I could ever have. He'll never know how much faith was built up in me simply by allowing me to participate in spite of my handicap. What a privilege to have a chance to make a come back. Monty Stratton was the first man to ever play professional ball with an artificial leg. But, to the best of my knowledge I was the first or one of the first to ever play college baseball with one. Many people think that when you are handicapped that you only want to prove something if you're trying to beat the odds. Or that you're just trying to bring attention to yourself. But really you just want to be like everybody else. The desires that are inside of you are just as real as the desires in someone that isn't handicapped. You begin to look at things with a little different perspective. But, you have to come to a point where you say, I'm not just going to live with this obstacle, I'm going to overcome it. I'm not going to sit back and let it devour my dreams because I'm going to accomplish them. If you can overcome the depression, the loneliness and the fear, then you have just made your first giant step toward victory. Everyday life is a challenge to all of us, but how willing are you to make your dreams come true. There is an old saying, "I can't, never did anything." Make your dreams come true. For, with God all things are possible to them that believe.

I remember going into a restaurant one time where there was a man sitting with his wife. It was immediately obvious that he had lost one of his legs. You could tell by the look on his face that he was a very bitter man. I walked up to his table and said,

"Excuse me sir, could I ask you a question?"

"He said, "What is it?"

"How long has it been since you lost your leg?" He told me and I said, "Have you been fitted with a new leg?"

"That's none of your business," he said.

The feeling of compassion I had for him was far greater than the embarrassment of his remark to me. So, I proceeded to tell him that I really did want to know. Then his wife burst in on the conversation and said,

"He received an artificial leg many years ago but he's too afraid to wear it."

I looked at him and said,

"Sir, did you know you are not the only one with that problem?"

As I said that, I reached down and hit my own artificial leg. The man broke down in tears and I was able to spend the next hour talking to him about the love of Jesus. It was wonderful to be able to share with him that he wasn't alone, that

God really did care. Each day I count it a privilege to tell others that we serve a God of miracles, a God that is more than able. We have got to remember that in spite of our present dreams being shattered and in spite of our broken hearts, tomorrow is a new day and another great opportunity to serve the Lord.

One night while I was still in college a group of us went to a Church of God outside of Dearborn, Michigan to hold a service. When it was time for the altar invitation, I sang the song, "A Crippled Boy's Prayer", it goes like this.

A little boy sat alone in a wheelchair
Watching all the other kids run and play
On his face I saw a look far in the distance
And yet I heard that little boy say,

They say you must be "Born Again" to enter Heaven
To walk the straight and narrow path on this earth
But Lord I don't seem to understand the meaning
I haven't walked since the day of my birth.

Lord, Will I be a crippled boy up in Heaven
Will my wings refuse to sail through the air
Lord, I know the way I am, is for a reason
But will I be a crippled boy up there?

His head was bowed, his little face was turned toward Heaven
Will my life there be the same, I heard him say

Through tears of joy his face lit up, He found
the answer
He turned to me, I heard that little boy say,

Lord, no I won't be a crippled boy in Heaven
I know my wings, well they will sail up through
the air
Lord, I know the way I am, is for a reason
But will I be a crippled boy up there?

Written by Steve Sanders

After I finished singing, I watched a little boy in the second row who was about nine or ten years old, reach down and pick up a pair of crutches. I had never noticed them before, but he began making his way up to the altar. His name was Billy and he had two braces on that he had worn since birth. He knelt down in front of me at the altar and as we both began to pray, he asked Jesus to come into his life and into his heart. In a couple of minutes his mother and father and the pastor came up and stood behind him and with tears streaming down his face he looked up at me and said,

"Preacher Mike, is it true that one day, I will get to run and play with all of the other kids, will I have new legs?"

I looked at Billy and began to cry and said,

"Billy that song is very true, if I can do it, you can too."

Before the service was over the Holy Spirit spoke to me and I told Billy, his parents and the pastor what the Lord said.

"Billy the Lord just told me that He is going to give you a miracle."

And Billy replied, "I know it, and I want you to promise me that in one year, you will come back so I can show you something."

Well of course, a year later I went back to that church and it was crowded to the max. I looked for Billy everywhere but I couldn't see him, so I just went on with the service. When I got to the point of the service when I was going to sing the "Crippled Boys Prayer" again, I saw Billy stand up in the back of the room where he had been hiding. Everyone else knew that he was there and he moved out into the center aisle and stood there without any crutches. I watched in amazement as I saw Billy begin to walk down the aisle. As he walked by every pew, people began to raise their hands and cry and weep with joy and thanksgiving for what the Lord had done. When Billy got to the front he walked up to me with tears in his eyes and with tears streaming down my face, I watched him as he raised up both of his pant legs. The braces that had been on Billy the last time I saw him were gone, because Jesus had healed him one year before. I was so excited to see God do a miracle in someone else's life, like He had done in mine. Billy's life had been changed, because we dared to believe what God had spoken that night. I never knew Billy's last name, but I know that there have been many like him that I've had the chance to meet over the years.

***

"Trust in the Lord

with all thine heart;

and lean not

unto thine own understanding.

In all thy ways

acknowledge Him,

and He will direct

your paths.

Proverbs 3:5,6

***

Chapter Six

LET GO AND LET GOD

As you might recall, I hadn't seen my natural father since I was four years old. Even though I was fortunate to have a good step-father whom I grew to love and respect, I was never able to totally put my natural father out of my mind. Mom had so many bad memories from the past that she was very adamant about him not being a part of our lives. To some degree she was totally right in keeping us from him. Oddly enough though, the desire to see him again just grew stronger the older I became. However, I wanted to please mom so I didn't pursue it until 1971. But by then, I had already had my accident and had made my come back on the baseball team. To my surprise I found out that he had been keeping "tabs" so to speak on me all of my life. He always tried to keep contact with someone in the family that would keep him updated. I was told that he wanted to be with me when I had my accident. But, mom wouldn't allow him to come around. I don't blame her for that, she was doing what she thought was best, but I couldn't help but feel like there was something missing in my life.

After becoming a man, I felt like I was capable of making my own decisions where my natural father was concerned. I contacted him and told him how anxious I was to see him. It had been sixteen years since I had talked to him. Can you imagine the excitement in the air, just knowing that we would soon be reuniting after all that time. The day after I made arrangements to see him my two older sisters called me up and asked if I would wait until New Years Eve to go see our father. I said no because I wanted to spend some time with him alone. Somehow though I allowed them to talk me into waiting. It was a decision I learned to regret. On Christmas morning we were all gathered at home when I heard the phone ring from my room. My dad went to answer it and came into the room with a look of gloom on his face. He said with tears in his eyes,

"I'm sorry Michael, but we've just gotten word that your father had a heart attack and he passed away in the middle of the night."

"Oh, God No," I cried out.

I burst out in tears and must have cried for the longest time. I was angry at my sisters for asking me to wait and I was angry at God for letting it happen. Another shattered dream and broken heart. Why did he have to die? I didn't even get to see him one last time. I just wanted to see what he looked like and what he had been doing all of these years. I wanted to share with him about how I grew up and how the Lord had come into my life. It would have been great to tell him about all my dreams and desires that I had for my future. I even wanted to be able to pour my heart out to him about the accident and maybe experience the understanding and compassion that only he could give me. Yet, there was no chance of that happening now. All those years were gone and now all of our future together as well. Until I saw him at his funeral, I didn't even know what he looked like or what kind of man he turned out to be. It was a very difficult day but I was able to meet a lot of people from his side of the family that I never knew existed. That helped me because I became friends with some of them and it gave me a very needed link to my father. Most of the time, children suffer severely when there is a separation between two parents. Often they are never free to establish the continued bond that they so desperately need with both parents. It's like having part of the pieces to a puzzle but knowing you can't seem to find the rest of the pieces to finish the picture. And, when this happens it usually leaves a long lasting feeling of emptiness. Nevertheless, life will go on either with the total picture or without it.

The year had not ended as I had expected but I knew I had to get on with things. I went back to college that fall where I stayed for one more year. Even before I went into full time ministry though, God was finding ways of using my life to help others. Doctor Leslie Bodnar called me one day and said,

"Michael would you be willing to meet with a young man who was injured in an accident? I'm not really sure what to say to him."

Timmy was in the same hospital that I had been in and he was only eleven years old so I told the doctor that I would help in anyway that I could. Timmy had been riding his bicycle on the sidewalk when suddenly he hit a pot hole. His bike fell over and Timmy stumbled into the street. Before he even had a chance to get out of the way, a semi-truck ran over his leg. Little Timmy of course was rushed to the hospital but all chances of saving his leg were gone. Timmy was so distraught that neither his parents or the doctor knew what to do. He began to go through severe withdrawal symptoms. He wouldn't speak to anyone and didn't respond to anything. He gave all of the outward appearances of someone who just wanted to die.

As I arrived at the hospital, I asked the Lord, "What am I going to say to this young boy?" And God said, "You've been there, you know what to do, and I'll guide you." As I went into the room his parents excused themselves and I sat down in a chair next to Timmy's bed. He was staring up at the ceiling as if he was in his own little world, not caring or acknowledging that anyone was in the room. I didn't say hi, how are you or anything, I just went in and sat down. I picked up my Bible and I read it for two hours and then I just quietly left. I came back everyday and did the same thing for four days. On the fifth day I didn't come back anymore. On the sixth day Timmy turned to his mom and said,

"Who was that man that came into my room everyday at the same time? He never said a word to me, he just read his Bible and prayed."

Timmy's mother told him all about me and I eventually started coming back to see him and we became very good friends. Soon though it was time to put my focus back on college and my preparations for ministry. I called Timmy and said, "I'm coming back to see you one more time." While we were alone in the hospital room together, he looked at me and said,

"Are you ever going to play sports again?"

I said, "I hope so Timmy."

" Well if you can, then I can too," he said with excitement. "You just wait and see, I'm going to be the next one to play.

He was so excited and bubbly about his plans for the future and I couldn't help but be excited for him.

Three weeks later, I received another phone call from Dr. Bodnar in which he said,

"Michael there has been a reversal in Timmy's recovery. Would you please come and explain to him that we're going to have to remove the rest of his leg because of an infection that has begun to spread up his thigh.

I said, "Doc, why can't you tell him, anyone but me."

But I realized that God still wanted to use me where Timmy was concerned. When I arrived at the hospital, I stood out in the hall for a few minutes watching the nurses go back and forth in his room. Finally, I walked through the door and saw Timmy laying there with a look of excitement on his face when he saw that it was me. It made me feel so good to see him happy that it brought tears to my eyes.

He said, "What are you doing here?"

"I've come back to see you for a little while Timmy, is that alright ?"

"Sure", he said with a sparkle in his eyes.

"Timmy, I've come to tell you something, that I think you already know. The doctors are going to have to remove more of your leg that might include your thigh, or you're going to die."

I saw the smile on Timmy's face quickly fade and tears began to well up in his eyes, as he turned his little head away from me. By then, my own tears had already begun to flow. Then with a look of extreme discouragement he turned around and looked at me and said,

"That means I'll never be able to do what you've been able to do, doesn't it?"

I said, "Timmy you can do anything that you want to do, it's just going to be a little more difficult."

Then with a twinkle of hope he said, "Do you think that I'll still be able to play sports?"

With all the faith that I could muster up I said, "We're going to pray that you will Timmy."

As I walked out of that room I said, "God forgive me, for all the times I complained about my situation and please help Timmy to be an overcomer in life."

All of us go through problems and trials and we think sometimes that it is the end of the world. In fact for many of us we become like the poster that says, "When you get to the end of the rope, tie a knot and hang on." We've all tied our knots and we've all hung on. But, there is a new poster that says, "When you get to the end of the rope, Let go and let God." You can't do anything, unless God helps you do it. I had done all that I knew to do for Timmy, now it was totally in God's hands. I said, "God the next time I start to complain, remind me that there are others who are going through a lot more pain and a lot more hurt than I have ever experienced."

I can happily tell you, that the next time I saw Timmy he was grown and had a few rewarding stories to tell me. He had already played high school baseball as the first baseman, his junior and senior years of school. I can't even express to you, how overwhelmed I was to see how God had performed in Timmy's life. Timmy had taken his "SHATTERED DREAMS AND BROKEN HEART" and allowed God to turn it all around.

There are many of you that might be reading this book right now, that are ready to give up just like Timmy and I were. But, I want you to know that you are not alone. You aren't the first person that's ever felt like giving up, and you won't be the last. But it's only when we "Let go, and let God", that the real miracles happen. He'll change our circumstances, when He can change us. What a testimony, what words of encouragement, what a blessing to know that God is still on the throne and able to turn all of our disasters into triumphs, if we will let Him.

I've often thought, I knew God's mercy
Was more that I could expect
And then all of a sudden, I realized
I haven't begun to touch it yet.

His heart is so much bigger
Than my imagination can see
And His total understanding
Far surpasses me.

He views the picture much more clearly
Than I, could ever hope I would
And even in my darkest hour
He's always understood.

If we'd just learn to trust Him
And take Him at His word
And let the Holy Spirit
Be the guiding voice we've heard.

Then when the test and trials
Start to come our way
We can rest with the assurance
That everything will be O.K.

He said, "He'll never leave us"
A precious promise, that is true
Whatever the situation
He will always see you through.

Copyright 1995 Victoria Lee

***

" His anger endureth

but for a moment

and in His favor is life.

Weeping endureth

for the night,

But joy

comes in the morning.

Psalm 30:5

***

Chapter Seven

JOY COMES IN THE MORNING

As a young single man traveling, I was searching for what God's purpose and direction was in my life concerning the ministry. I began to fast and pray and ask God what He wanted me to do and who He wanted me to be with. I realized that I had a lot to learn and my desire to do His will was so important. The ministry was fairly new to me and I had no idea that along with all the blessings would also come pitfalls. Little did I realize at the time that God would take even the pitfalls and work them out for His glory if I would let Him.

I found myself headed up to Colorado in the summer of 1972. I had been invited to a little church in South Denver for the Wednesday night service with Reverend Jackson. It was there that I met my future wife Gracelynn. I decided to preach a few extra days there so that we could spend more time together. Then by the end of the weekend, I had decided that she must be the one that God had brought my way. We became engaged in September of '72 and in December we decided to go back to Michigan so she could meet my parents. Then, in January 1973 we had a beautiful formal church wedding which began our exciting life together, one full of memories that we could both share. Our enthusiasm was overwhelming. In spite of all the past few years that had been filled with disappointments, I was on my way to a wonderful life, with a beautiful wife.

After our wedding, I decided to enter Central Bible College in Springfield, Missouri. I also worked for Burger King to make ends meet and was quite an asset to the company in helping build up their restaurant. The franchise owner was so impressed with me that when he came into town he bought me a new car. Many times when it was rough going in the ministry I would think back about the future I might have had in the restaurant business. That's another time when you realize your calling because believe me, the money was far better managing a restaurant than it was ministering in churches. Also there was less chance of backbiting, jealousy and rumors in a restaurant setting. But, I knew what God had called me to do.

I was in school for one semester and getting ready to go into the fall semester of '73 when we decided to move back to Colorado. During the next several months I received a settlement for my accident and the loss of my leg.

Before I left school, I remember one of my professors telling me that Bible College was only about nine or ten percent of the ministry. He said the real test of your calling was when you would fall down in life and be willing to get up and try again. If you know your purpose then nothing can hold you back. You'll be able to withstand any trial or test that comes before you. Because, you'll know that God will see you through. The Bible says, what God has foreordained, He has predestined. In other words, He has the Master Plan. All you have to do is follow it. But, He always gives you the choice. Plan A - is God's way and it will lead you into His perfect will.

Gracelynn and I were still so new in the ministry and we had no idea what the future had in store. We traveled all across America doing crusades and a lot of church revival meetings. God was teaching and preparing us for all the days that lie ahead. We saw tremendous blessings happen in every meeting He took us to. People were being saved, healed and restored everywhere we went. The power of the Holy Spirit was evident in all of our meetings throughout the country. We knew that God wanted to use us and it filled our hearts with so much joy. Then one day in November of 1974 Gracelynn experienced her first miscarriage. It would be the first of three that she would go through. But, we were still confident that God would give us children.

Finally, our prayers were answered and on February 14, 1976 Carrieann Elizabeth Shaw entered the world. What better gift could Gracelynn and I receive on Valentine's Day than a token of our love together, the birth of our first child. I knew from the time that she was born, that she was very special. I knew that God was going to use her some day. Many nights when she was little, I would sit up late rocking her and singing to her and telling her how special she was, until she fell asleep.

Once in the summer of '76 when the big Thompson Canyon Flood happened, we were scheduled to go up there to minister and sing. Just two days before we were to head back home, we spent some time with our friends after the evening service. As we were driving home afterwards, Gracelynn was at the wheel and Carrieann was sound asleep between us. I had just reached down and put my hand on her when suddenly our car was hit from behind by a semi-truck. It knocked us about one hundred and fifty yards from the point of impact. Gracelynn's seat belt was literally ripped loose from the floor and the seat. They rushed us to the hospital and thank God all of us were alright. I just had a bump on my head from hitting the broken windshield, but I remember how scared I was at the thought of losing my family and just how close we had come to doing just that.

Several months had gone by and we had been living in Colorado when I received a phone call from my sister Linda. She was tearfully explaining to me that mom was in the hospital and they thought she was dying. She said that during a biopsy conducted by the doctor's a couple of weeks earlier, that they had accidentally punctured an artery behind her liver. For the past couple of weeks, she had been bleeding internally. They were getting ready to take her into surgery in the next few minutes.

"You better come home quick Michael," she said. "The doctors don't think that she will make it out of surgery alive because she has lost so much blood."

With my throat so choked up I could hardly talk, I told Linda that I would be on the next plane out of town. As tears filled my eyes, I thought to myself, "I can't lose mom."

The next four hours were to be the longest of my life, even longer than the time of preparing for the loss of my leg. Arriving at the hospital I looked at faces that were sad and crying in the waiting room. My oldest sister Linda came up and hugged me and told me that mom had survived, but she wasn't expected to make it through the night.

"She's in the intensive care unit," she said.

Making my way down the hall, all I could think about was that I was going to lose the one person who meant the most to me. Besides my wife and family, mom was the main focus of my life and she could soon be gone forever.

Standing at the intensive care unit, I began to look in and I saw just one bed that was being used that night, and that was the bed that was holding my mother. Entering the room, I motioned to the nurse and made my way to my mother's bed. I could hardly recognize her as she laid there unconscious with her face white and ashen and pale. Tubes were going into her body in several places as they were trying to replace all of the blood that she had lost.

Growing up as the only boy in the family, you have a certain bond with your mother that is different from everyone else. Mom and I used to have a little way of saying hello to each other and it was also our way of saying "I Love You!" Whenever I would be gone and she knew that I was coming home on a certain day, she would always come and sit or stand looking down the road from our house waiting to see me drive up and then she knew I was alright and home safely. I could cause her to worry a lot because of my traveling and because she never knew what I was going to do next. When I came in and saw her standing at the window, I would come up behind her and whisper in her ear, "Mama, I'm home and I love you!" "I love you too," she would say and then we would hug. I remember looking down at her and thinking Lord she can't die yet, she hasn't lived long enough and then I whispered in her ear, "Mama, I'm here and I love you!"

I must have whispered it a couple of times, when suddenly her head started to move and her eyes began to flicker. When she opened her eyes, even the nurse was startled and said I have to report this right away. She then came back and stood by the bed as mom and I began to talk. But the nurse never said a word, she would just nod from time to time. When we prayed, she bowed her head and prayed with us and said Amen.

"I told them to tell you not to come," she said.

"Why mom," I said softly with tears in my eyes.

"Because what you are doing is more important than me," she whispered.

I couldn't believe it, for the first time my mother had finally told me that she approved of what I was doing in my life and you will never know what that meant to me. I had always grown up wanting the approval of my parents and as a young preacher it was even more important. I used to long for the day when my mom and dad would come to a ball game and sit in the stands and watch me play. I used to picture in my mind, what it would be like to look up in the stands like all the other guys and see my parents sitting there and cheering me on, but it seldom ever happened. But it seemed like I could always count on mom, as my biggest secret fan, and that meant a lot to me. Yet, here she was telling me now, that it wasn't important for me to be there with her.

"Mom, I love you very much and you're not going to die," I said. "In fact mom, I want you to pray a prayer with me that will make sure that you are going to be alright."

"Will you pray with me?", I said and she nodded her head to me, but I will never forget her words just before we prayed. She said,

"Just pray so that no one hears you."

I thought to myself, "God forgive us for being ashamed to acknowledge you."

In the next few moments, I prayed the sinners prayer which I asked her to pray with me. It's a prayer of salvation to ask Jesus to come into your life and dwell there. When we were finished I said, "Mom did you pray that prayer with me?" "Yes I did," she whispered and the nurse and I both cried because we knew that mom had come home and that death could not harm her any longer. "Mom, I'm going to pray another prayer and I want you to believe with me." It was almost like she knew what I was going to pray, because before I could say another word, she said,

"Just pray that the good Lord will take care of your dad and your sisters and I'll be OK."

"Mom this is what the Lord has given me the opportunity to do for many people and that is to pray with them that they will be healed in the name of Jesus."

As we began to pray, something began to happen and you could feel the atmosphere change in that room. Even the nurse said later that she felt something dark and heavy leave and I agreed. We both felt that death had left and that the Lord was going to heal her that night.

The next morning, we received a call from the doctor. When he talked to me on the phone he asked what had happened the night before. When I told him, there was silence and then he said,

"Whatever it was, it worked because your mother's blood count is normal and she is walking around this morning. She is also eating and we have run tests on her and all we can say is that a miracle has happened.

At the hospital a couple of days later I asked mom if she knew what had happened and she told me yes. She said she was glad that she had accepted the Lord into her life and glad that He had healed her. That was a new beginning for mom, a brand new relationship with the Lord Jesus Christ.

After we knew mom was on the road to recovery, I also needed to get back on the road of ministry. Remember, I had a full schedule that the Lord had so graciously given me. I felt even more prepared now than before after experiencing God's healing power toward mom.

We began having some tremendous revival meetings and the Holy Spirit was evident in every one of them. I had just finished a week of meetings in Richmond, Missouri when I had an experience that I'll never forget. It was on a Sunday night and I had come out to the foyer to shake hands with the people. Suddenly someone tapped me on the shoulder and as I turned around there stood a young man. His countenance was so very brilliant that I thought to myself, "Why haven't I seen this man before?" When you are ministering you always look out into the audience and you see who all the people are. But, I knew that I had not seen him.

He said, "Do you have a minute?"

I said, "Yes Sir."

"I have to give you a message from the Lord. He told me to tell you that the enemy is going to try and take your life tonight on the way home."

Rather than think that the man was crazy, I had to believe that God was using him to speak to me. He looked at me again and said,

"Did you understand what I said?"

"Yes" I said, but tell me again.

He said, "The only word I can tell you is the word CAR."

With a puzzled look I turned to look at some of the other people and as I turned back around, he was gone. The door that was close to us, had not been moved and when I went outside to see if I could find him, he was nowhere in sight. Nobody saw him leave, so I had to believe that it was an angel that the Lord had sent to me. That night stands vividly out in my mind, it was late August of 1977. The pastor and some of the other congregation gathered around me to pray and pleaded with me not to leave, but I left anyway.

I was crossing the Topeka Turnpike when suddenly I was on the C.B. talking to a truck driver in front of me. I was also talking to a station wagon that was behind me and then I decided to pass the truck as we went down in the valley. As we came up over the top of the hill, I saw headlights that looked like they were break lights dead center in the road. My first thought was, I have a truck and a station wagon behind me and I'm pulling a trailer so I better pull to the right. As I tried to pull to the right, I went to the left instead. Immediately, because of the snow on the ground I slid into the center of the median and the trailer flipped over and blew everything out. The car spun around and around but it never flipped over. As I sat there in the car while it was smoldering and smoking, I heard a voice say,

"Get out of the car and walk over to the side," which I did.

The truck driver, his partner and the four people from the station wagon came running over to me to see if I was alright. I looked over the side of the road and saw a forty foot embankment straight down and I know my heart must have skipped a beat. If I had of gone to the right instead of the left, I would have been dead. I was so thankful to the Lord for saving my life that night and it quickly reminded me of another time and another place with such similar circumstances. Back in 1971, just two years after I had lost my leg and had my artificial leg, I was driving home after church one night. I had driven this way at least a thousand times before but this time as I was coming around a curve passing a truck weigh station, I must have fallen asleep. When I woke up, I saw that I had moved from the first lane to the fourth lane. I was literally off the road and I was headed right for a steel reflector and I jerked the car to the right at the last minute. It severed 13 inches of steel reflector which came right through the windshield and bounced down and hit my right leg, the artificial one. Of course if it would have hit my good leg it would have gone clear through it, but instead it hit the brace. The car flipped over a number of times and subsequently I was rushed to the hospital. Many pieces of shattered glass had to be pulled out of each one of my eyes, and I laid in the hospital bed for a week unable to see. I remember saying, "Dear God, why are these things happening to me. Why have I gone through so many trials?" And again the Lord said, "Be still, in spite of it all you're in preparation."

So with now the second near death experience on the highway, I knew God was continually watching over me. When I got back home we had to purchase a new van but I was able to use the other car as a trade in. You aren't going to believe this, but within 48 hours of that accident I was in another one on my way to Arizona. But the Lord spared my life there also. I have often told people that I have nine lives, of which I've used up about seven or eight of them.

***

One night in the fall of 1977, God gave me a vision. Gracelynn and I were in a couple's home during a week of meetings and I woke up and I was in a cold sweat. I turned on the television and there was a movie that was just about to end. The couple in the movie was driving down the road in a car and the woman was singing "Joy Comes in the Morning." The man started singing with her also and when they were finished he turned to her and said,

"Where does that song come from?",

She said, "The Bible, Psalm 30:5"

I immediately opened my Bible and there it was.

"His anger endureth but for a moment.
In His favor is life.

Weeping may endure for the night, but
joy comes in the morning."

I wrote down the vision of all the things to come that God gave me that night. He showed me a ministry that He would one day call me to build and be a part of. It was the ministry of Restoration. I'll never forget the vision, because it came to me in a dream. Suddenly I was shown the property and as I looked over it, I saw a building that was very beautiful. The property had meadows and it had a white fence all around it. It had a lake in the front with a fountain and a garden. Behind that was a building and a facility and I saw the inside and the outside. When I went around to the back I saw a lot of housing and parking lots.

I asked the Lord, "What is the housing for?" and He said, "This is to take care of all the fallen ministries one day, where broken hearted people will come to be ministered to and restored."

I remember going inside of the building and there were T.V. cameras and radio coverage and the auditorium was filled. There were three to four thousand people there. I saw 34 ministers in the front and they were all praising God.

I said, "Lord who are these ministers?" and He said, "They are many of the well known ministers and leaders that have fallen."

I said, "But Lord where is the shepherd?" and He said, "It is you."

I was in a cold sweat and I woke up. I had never even been a senior pastor, yet God was showing me that I would be the shepherd of all these people. I thought God this sounds crazy. Surely you don't mean me.

Gracelynn and I spent a lot of time that year praying for God's direction in our lives. We sat down and made a list of everything that we wanted him to do for us and with us in the coming year. We thought 1978 would be our year of "New Beginnings." So, that's what we called it. We were going to believe that God would do things for our ministry that we had always wanted.

Oddly enough, even in a denomination where people are known for being open to the move of the Holy Spirit, we sometimes find people and even pastors who have a hard time understanding.

I'm reminded of an incident in Lima, Ohio where I was ministering. The power of God was so strong in that little church and people were extremely hungry to see God move in a miraculous way. When we freely allow the Holy Spirit to enter our services, he opens doors and reveals things that have sometimes been shut and hidden for a long time. So it was at this church, on a lively Sunday morning. The deacons began dancing around the room hugging each other and asking one another for forgiveness of one thing or the other. A lot of bondage's were being broken off of people and the love of God was being poured out all over the room. To my dismay though, the pastor came up to me after the service and said,

"Brother Mike, I don't believe in all of those things, so we are going to have to close down the meetings."

I couldn't believe my ears, I again was shattered at the thought of grieving the Holy Spirit in such a way.

That afternoon I phoned another pastor in Northern Ohio. After relating to him what had just occurred, he invited me to come on to his church and continue what God had started. So, that Sunday night we were at a different church but with the same anointing. It was wonderful to see how the Lord was so ready to save, heal and deliver people that would hunger and thirst after Him. Monday night the anointing had gotten even stronger and by Tuesday we were jumping for joy.

After the services Tuesday night Gracelynn and I went back to our motel room. She was sitting on the bed with Carrieann and I had sat down at the desk where the T.V. was, and with the remote in my hand I began to sort of channel surf. While doing this, I ran across the 700 Club with Pat Robertson and Ben Kinchlow and just as I was about to flip the channel again, I heard Pat say, "Don't touch that dial." I turned and looked at Gracelynn and she smiled and said, "He's got you doesn't he?" So I left it on there for a moment and they started praying. He said,

"There is a preacher that is listening tonight that needs a miracle."

I thought to myself, "Well yes Lord, we need a miracle but there is probably 20,000 other preachers listening that need one as well."

As they continued to pray, Ben stopped and said,

"That preacher is in a motel room right now."

I looked at Gracelynn and she looked at me and I thought wow, this is something. That narrows it down to about 5,000 preachers that possibly might be listening. Finally, they prayed a few minutes longer and then Pat said,

"That preacher is in the state of Ohio."

I thought wow. And then Ben said,

"And they're in bed and I want them to get out of bed and on their knees right now."

I looked at Gracelynn and she looked at me and we immediately fell on our knees and began to pray. While we were praying, the power of God covered our room. I'll never forget what Pat said that night. He said, "The answer is on the way, so go to bed now and go to sleep because it's going to be the best nights rest that you have ever had." Sure enough I went to bed and went straight to sleep.

The next morning the phone rang and on the other end was a lady by the name of Lynn Robbins. She said,

"Michael I'm the assistant director for PTL Ministries. Jim Baker wants you to come and minister at PTL.

I thought that she was joking so I hung up on her. Well, she called back and again she shared the same thing. She said,

"Michael we would like for you to come next week."

"Well I can't come next week because I'm still in a meeting."

"Well" she said, "When is your next available time?"

We decided on November 20, 1978. Believe me we were on cloud nine waiting for that day to come. We finished up the meeting we were in and continued on to another church that had already been scheduled. After that meeting the pastor and his wife asked if they could go with us to PTL. The Praise The Lord Club was just starting and had begun to spread all over the country and everyone was anxious to be a part of it. I remember as we entered the PTL property the presence of God was felt so strongly. This of course was before all the scandals started and God was blessing them in a mighty way.

Lynn Robbins took me into a room and began interviewing me so that she would have a clearer understanding about my testimony. About half way through the interview, she excused herself and came back a few seconds later with Uncle Henry Harrison who was Jim Baker's right hand man. After a few minutes he excused himself and came back with someone else. Before I knew it, I was sharing my story with a room full of people that were crying and weeping over everything I said. Finally Uncle Henry came over to me and said,

"Michael, God is going to bless your testimony tomorrow when people hear it across America."

After showing us around parts of the property and taking a few pictures, we all returned back to the studio. The piano player Paul had just come in and we introduced ourselves. I told him I was going to be on the program and I had a song that I wanted to sing, called "A Crippled Boy's Prayer". It was wonderful practicing with Paul because he was so sensitive to what God was doing in my life.

The next morning when we arrived at PTL to be on the program, Gracelynn went and sat on the front row with the audience. I was in the back behind the curtains. Dr. C.M. Ward and a couple of other major ministries were also waiting to come on the program, along with a man that was unable to appear the day before, due to a lack of time. I was sitting in the very back of the room just waiting to be called, feeling so grateful to even be there. I thought I probably wouldn't get on the program until the second hour since there were major ministries that were also there. PTL was doing two hours of taping, one was live in which 65 million people would see it and the other one was taped and sent around the country to be viewed. I thought to myself,

"Lord why would you bring me here if we're going to be on the second hour where no one will see it live? I know it's an opportunity but I'm asking you to open a door so that this testimony can touch the lives of people like never before."

Well that day Tammy sang her song "Blessed Assurance" and while she was singing the Holy Spirit spoke to Jim and said have me come on first. Now whatever feelings you might have about Jim or Tammy now, try to remember that in the beginning of their ministry God was very much alive and apart of what they were doing. It was obvious from the moment that you walked onto the PTL premises. Lynn Robbins came back behind the curtains and said,

"Michael you're on first."

I yelled out, "You mean in front of C.M.Ward." He is one of the great ministers of our generation, the head of Revival Times for the Assemblies of God for over twenty five years. He turned and said,

"Michael this is your hour and God's hour, share it for the kingdom of God."

As I went out, Jim began to ask questions and normally in the studio there are a lot of other things that are going on at the same time. But on this day, the Holy Spirit moved in a mighty way.

They had a slew of phones in the background that were normally lit up constantly but during my testimony the phones did not ring because people were obviously listening to my testimony all over America. I remember seeing Tammy and the PTL singers kneeling down with tears streaming down their faces, unable to finish with their song. You could have heard a pin drop in that place because the power of God was so strong. Jim was crying, Uncle Henry was crying and the Spirit of God was moving. When we finished the first hour, I was still the first guest. Jim said,

"How many of you want to continue with this testimony?"

And hands went up all over the room. So when we finished the first hour, I realized that God had answered my prayer. Over sixty-five million people had seen Michael Shaw for the first time and heard the testimony that God had given me. A testimony of how God could do a miracle in someone's life. About how He could change them and restore their dreams and mend their broken heart.

When we went into the second hour I was the only guest on the set except for Jim's brother and then Dr. C.M. Ward in the last few minutes of the program. Along with my testimony I shared with the audience the vision that God had given me concerning the ministry of Restoration. I told them that our churches were going to be filled with people that have been hurt and destroyed. Little did I know, what a prophetic word that was. Dr. Ward said,

"Jim in all the years that I've been on T.V. this is one of the most powerful messages and testimonies that I've ever heard."

After the program was over, I decided to stay at the studio for a while so we could man the phones and pray with people. It was amazing to talk to so many people that had given their hearts to the Lord after hearing my testimony. I was overwhelmed at the tremendous response of people from all across America. Around three o'clock in the morning the pastor that had come with me suggested that maybe we should get on back to our wives at the motel. So the two of us said our good-byes and headed out the door.

We sort of got side tracked though when we both realized that it had been a long night and we were both hungry. I wanted to go to one restaurant and he suggested another one that I wasn't particularly fond of, but he talked me into it. No sooner had we gotten inside, until people started coming up to me and saying,

"Hey aren't you the guy on the television."

I looked up and there it was, PTL being played around the clock. I'd never had this kind of notoriety before, people were wanting me to pray for them right there in the restaurant. A young man who had been sitting in the back came up to me and started crying. He said,

"You are an answer to prayer."

I looked at him and thought, "What in the world are you talking about." I looked at pastor Ron and he smiled at me and said,

"See, I told you we should come here."

Then the young man said,

"After watching your program I got a call from Germany and my sister was in an automobile accident. She was hit by a train and she's in the hospital, they want to remove her legs or she's going to die. I talked with her and begged and pleaded, but she won't let them do it. So, I came here to the restaurant where I usually come at night to study and I said , "God I'm not leaving until you bring Michael Shaw here to give me and answer."

So there I was, Michael Shaw at 3:30 in the morning in a little restaurant that I didn't even want to be at, talking to a man that was convinced now that God was real. He said,

"Will you pray for my sister?"

So right there we began to pray and instead of people standing around mocking and laughing, they began to pray with us. The man excused himself and in a few minutes he returned and said,

"Brother Mike, I have my sister on the phone in Germany, would you please talk to her."

I couldn't believe this was happening, just because of a television broadcast about me. I went to the phone and for forty-five minutes I talked to her about Jesus Christ and what He can do in your life. I asked her if she realized the damage to her legs and she said yes. So, I said, "What are you waiting for?"

Shortly after that phone conversation it was reported that she did have her legs removed and I heard later that she learned to walk again. Praise God, what sometimes seems like the end, is just the beginning if we will let go, and let God.

Our introduction to the PTL family was the beginning of an explosion for our ministry. Pastors from everywhere were calling us to come and minister at their churches. They were calling me instead of me having to call them and that was somewhat of a relief. Remember the list that Gracelynn and I had made, asking God to grant us? Well the last one on the list to be fulfilled was, Lord cause this ministry to minister to millions of people for your kingdom and for your glory and he did it in just a few short hours.

For the next two years I was privileged to go back to PTL on a couple of occasions, which thrilled me to say the least. We had experienced a lot of rewarding times in the ministry and we knew that God still had a lot more in store for us.

***

"Jesus said unto her,

I am the Resurrection

and the Life;

he that believeth in Me,

though he were dead,

yet shall he live:

and whosoever liveth

and believeth in Me

shall never die.

Believeth thou this?"

John 11:25-26

***

Chapter Eight

IT'S NOT THE END, IT'S JUST THE BEGINNING

Life is a series of happenings and changes. Some fill you with a lot of joy while others can fill you with a lot of pain.

In 1981, we started a wonderful church called the Heritage Christian Center and many people were reached for Jesus during that time. We all grew to some extent in our walk with the Lord and things looked like they couldn't get any better. Then another shattered dream and broken heart became a reality.

Looking through the window at the street below, I could see both the world below me and I could see her reflection in the window. Down on the sidewalk a couple was walking hand in hand, not realizing that just above them in a hospital room lay a woman that was dying. According to her doctors, this woman, whose life was very precious to me, had only a few more hours to live.

They passed by and I could see them smiling. Maybe they were making plans for their future or talking about the day's events. Maybe they were in love and just making small talk and looking forward to the moments and the time that they would be together. Death did not appear to be a part of their vocabulary or a part of their lives at the time. Yet there would come a day when they too would have to face it themselves, either in their own lives or through the loss of a friend or family member. Maybe their moments together would be short lived and soon they would part never seeing each other again. They would only be memories in each others mind. Or maybe they were meant to be together and share a lifetime of hopes and dreams.

They never looked up from the street below and they never saw the sad and lonely figure looking back at them with tears in his eyes. Their movements as they walked away were replaced by the image and the reflection staring back at me through the window. Laying in a bed a few feet away was the one person that I had loved more than anyone else in this life.

Turning, I walked to the bed and tried to sit down on the edge while trying not to cry or show my real feelings. This was a time to be strong and a time to show her that I could deal with any situation in my life. Yet looking into those eyes and watching her try to smile that smile that she always gave me, was more than I could bear and I began to cry.

How could this happen, I thought to myself? Why was this taking place now Lord? Surely you can see the hurt and pain that I'm feeling and surely you can see the pain that she's in laying in that bed not knowing if she would see tomorrow. Yet there was silence and the voice that I had known for so many years, that had spoken and given me direction and wisdom and hope during other difficult times in my life, was now silent and only the sound of the fan could be heard filling the room.

For the past six years, we had gotten to have mom as a changed person who had experienced the Love of God in her life. The love that she had shown before was far greater now than it had ever been. I'll never forget that Christmas, when the family was sitting in the living room and all of the presents had been passed out. Mom told my sister that there was one more present that needed to be opened. When they brought it to me, everyone got real quiet. As I opened the box, I stopped and cried when the top came off and I looked down and saw my first set of Bible commentaries. When I looked up, everyone else including mom and dad were crying. I guess it's hard to understand why so many people would cry over a set of Bible Commentaries. But, what you don't know is that it took a lot for mom and dad to buy those books, a lot of hard work and most of all, a lot of love. Especially since dad was so much against my going into the ministry to begin with. This was one Christmas that I would never forget. It was like a huge stamp of approval for what God had called me to do.

Sitting next to mom on that hospital bed made me realize just how short life really is. The time that we do have with each other is precious and very important. There will come a day when those that we love and care about in life, will be gone. Only the memories will linger along with the hope of reuniting on that great and wonderful day of the Lord.

I said, "Mom have I ever failed you?"
I couldn't believe that I had just said that to her. Of course I had failed her. Of course I had caused her many a night's sleep and now all that I could do was wait for her answer. With tears in her eyes, she said,

"No Michael you haven't", I love you and I'm proud!"

At that moment, my little daughter Carrieann came into the room and crawled up on the bed and into Grandma's lap and said,

"Grandma, you can't leave yet, I haven't had enough of you and I don't want you to die."

There are some moments that you wish you could hold onto forever and this was one of them. It was as if God had planned this very moment. For within a few minutes, the door opened and one by one the family came into the room. I will never forget it, as long as I live. Something that I had asked the Lord to do for so long had now taken place. They all knelt beside her bed and began to pray.

Mama's kidneys had failed and she was bloating up with water. Then her liver started to fail and the doctor told us mom had a serious problem with colitis that would kill her, but that everyday that she continued to live gave her a better chance of survival. I found out later that he was the same doctor that had been there with her six years earlier. He said that he had become a Christian since then and when he went home that night, he promised that he and his wife would be praying for another miracle.

Miracles are some of the most beautiful things that God could ever create and bring to pass in a person's life. A miracle is totally dependent upon the Lord and yet the receiver must have faith and belief on their part to make it happen. Of course, they also need to realize that the situation is totally in the hands of the Lord.

There are many in the church and in the world, that can believe that everything that happens is because of coincidence or because man has the power within himself to make it happen. They can believe that it would be easier for us to have come from monkeys through evolution then to believe that there is a God in Heaven that is just waiting to show each of us that He loves us. And that He wants to do the impossible in our lives.

Many who claim to be Christians today, have a hard time believing that miracles still happen. They mock preachers who still believe in the words of the Lord and in the truths of the Bible. They call them faith healers and then make fun of them in the movies and in books and publications. How easy it has become for people to mock something, that they know very little about. Also, what they fail to realize, is that the greatest miracle that Jesus could ever do, is the miracle of salvation. When He comes into a person's life and forgives them of their sins and saves their soul, that's a miracle. When He can take a person that has called it silly all of their lives or a bunch of emotionalism, and by the move of the Holy Spirit cause them to change their mind in the twinkling of an eye, that's a miracle.

Those of us who are "Born Again", and have Jesus as part of our lives are very familiar with the transformation. And those who aren't ought to realize what a privilege it is to have the King of Kings take up residence in you. The Bible says, "That you don't choose Him, but He chooses You." Therefore, when the sweet Holy Spirit is dealing with you to accept Jesus into your life, please don't take that lightly. The Bible also says, "His Spirit won't always abide with you," and how do you know if He will ever pass your way again?" The presence of the Holy Spirit is the sweetest experience we'll ever know and nothing can come close to comparing with His Glory.

Listen to the words of the Lord found in John 14:12-14

"Verily, verily, I say unto you, he that believeth on me, the works that I do shall he do also, and greater works than these shall you do because I go to be with the Father. And whatsoever you shall ask in my name, that will I do, that the Father will be glorified in the Son. If you shall ask anything in my name, I will do it."

The Lord has promised each of us the same power and authority that He gave his disciples back then. Here are some more powerful scriptures that deal with this same area, that each of us needs to get a hold of for the completeness of our lives and belief as Christians.

Hebrews 13:8 - "Jesus Christ the same yesterday and today and forever."

We must remember that if Jesus stays the same, then His word and His promises and His Holy Spirit must also stay the same for each of us within our hearts and lives.

Matthew 17:20 - "Because of your unbelief, for verily I say unto you, If you had the faith as a grain of mustard seed, you would be able to say to the mountain, 'Remove to yonder place' and it would be moved and (nothing) shall be impossible with you."

Mark 11:24 - "Therefore I say unto you, what things so ever you desire, when you pray, believe that you will receive them, and you shall have them."

The problem with a lot of people, is that they find it easier to believe in themselves than they do in a loving and caring God. Jesus had been ministering for many days, when he received word that one of his best friends Lazarus had just died. The family Mary and Martha were distraught that the Lord had not come in time. So when Jesus got near to the home of Lazarus, they each ran out to meet him and questioned how he could be about healing other people and caring about other people's needs and wants, but not have time for their own and his best friend.

Yet when Jesus drew nigh, the very first thing that He did was to weep and show his love and his personal feelings for his best friend. Then he revealed to each of those individuals that were standing there that day, their lack of faith in Him and in the Father and in the teachings that he had given them over and over again.

It did not take the Lord very long to show the power that He possessed through the Father, as he spoke those words, "Lazarus, come forth." How many miracles does the Lord have to perform, before we are willing to believe that He is who He said that He is, the Son of God. It becomes much easier to blame God and to blame the Lord when things are not going the way that we want them to in life. Often we hear the words of the skeptic's cry out, "If God is such a loving God, then why are so many children and hurting people having to suffer and die in this world?"

Through all the crusades and all of the meetings, I have never been able to understand why many are healed, while others go away empty or in the same condition. People will make fun of the Benny Hinns and the Kathryn Kuhlman's and Oral Roberts and many others including myself, yet they do not understand the anointing and they truly don't understand the sovereignty of God and the working of the Holy Spirit.

If there is one key that unlocks the mystery of miracles, it is found in

Hebrews 11:1 - "Faith is the substance of things hoped for in life, and the evidence of things not always seen."

One of the greatest keys to receiving your miracle is found in the Word of God and in your walk and faith with the Lord Jesus Christ. I have discovered that the words to the song, "Only Believe" which they played the night I walked across the platform are the same words that people need to put into their minds and hearts. If you are ever going to see the hand of God move in a miraculous way in your life, you have to believe. It took believing to play college baseball with an artificial leg. And it will take believing for you to accomplish the impossible in your own life. But, you can't believe unless you know in whom you believe. Jesus Christ is the same yesterday, today and forever and His word is forever established. He is the Alpha and the Omega, the Beginning and the End. He is the Bright and Morning Star, the Rose of Sharon and The Lily of the Valley. In Him we can live and move and have our very existence. He wants you to be an overcomer in every area of your life. But you can only overcome if you believe that you can.

Sometimes its hard to believe when things are not going right in your life and in your circumstances. It's hard to picture in your mind that everything is going to work out when suddenly you are alone and facing your greatest obstacles in life. Yet it is during this time that God can prove himself to you and reveal His glory.

We need to establish "God Confidence". What I mean by that is confidence to believe that God is going to bring you through your circumstances. You can't always see the end from the beginning but it doesn't mean the end isn't there. God took Moses and the people of Israel through the wilderness for forty years. Not because it took forty years to cross the wilderness, because it was really only an eleven day trip. But it took forty years because there was a lot of preparation to do in the hearts of the people before they got to the promise land.

You may be going through some things right now that you just don't understand. You may be saying, "But God I thought you wanted me to do such and such or be such and such and yet it's been (forty years so to speak) and I haven't gotten there or become that yet." And I say to you, "Hold On", God is not finished with you yet. He said that He isn't a man that He could lie and that He changes not. He wants to change those forty years into eleven days if you'll let him. But there has to be a time of preparation to get you prepared for the great things that He has in store for you. Are you ready to have "God Confidence" no matter what your circumstances look like today? Are you ready to stand steadfast and believe God in spite of what you might see or not see? Can you truly say, "God is at my right hand, and I shall not be moved?" Then and only then will you begin to see those (symbolic forty years) turn into eleven days.

As I look back on so many years of my own life, I can see times of preparation that God was bringing me through. I share with you my defeats and disappointments only to point out to you my own struggles in my symbolic forty year walk. I do this in hopes, that you may learn from my experiences how to more readily have "God Confidence" for your SHATTERED DREAMS AND BROKEN HEARTS.

Watching and waiting for my mother to get better seemed to drain me and yet I knew that if God could heal her once, then He could do it again. Minutes turned into hours and hours into days. When I arrived back at the hospital a couple of days later, I knew that something was about to happen. Maybe everyone did that day, because we were all praying the same prayer, "Lord if you can not give her back the way she was, then take her home because she's ready to meet you now."

Entering the hospital, I asked where everyone was and they told me that they were scattered around different parts of the hospital praying for mom. When I went into her room she had slipped into another coma and had not woken up. I held her hand and looked at her pale face and I knew that it was time for the Lord to take her home. I remember thinking to myself, "Lord why don't you heal her?" And then I heard that voice again speaking inside of me saying, "It's alright, she's mine."

A few minutes later, mom opened her eyes and with my wife and sisters standing right there, she spoke these few words. "It's beautiful", and then she closed her eyes and with a slight smile on her face, she went home to be with the Lord.

Life for each of us is but a heartbeat in time. It's a moment in eternity that can pass quickly or last for what seems like almost forever. We live in a real world, with real problems and with hurting people. Yet there is a real God in Heaven, that tries everyday to reveal himself to each of us. He doesn't do it with gimmicks or magic or pulling rabbits out of our hats. He doesn't spend time trying to convince us that He is real, when He already did that on a place called Calvary almost two thousand years ago. Now He just simply wants us to believe.

We have a choice and a freedom to make decisions right or wrong in life and that is what separates us from being robots or machines or animals. The Lord gave us that choice at Calvary when He gave his only begotten Son for a lost world.

He knows where you are right now and He is not going to try and communicate with you through voodoo or reincarnation or horoscopes. He can not be your good luck charm or your special rabbits foot. He can not be the genie from the lamp that will give you three wishes and then disappear until you need Him again.

He is however the Alpha and the Omega and the Beginning and the End of everything that has to do with your life. He is the Author and the Finisher of your faith even when you don't feel like praying. He's the friend and brother that you never had in life and He wants to be closer to you than anyone you've ever known. He will be the one walking with you when you are alone and He will be standing beside you when no one else will.

You can listen and hear Him speaking to you everytime you take a breath and everytime you hear that voice inside you telling you what to do. It's not your conscience and its not a strange voice, but it is the voice of the living God, who cares about you and every situation that you are going through.

The next time you need a miracle, stop looking in the paper for a sign and forget about the 800 or 900 numbers, because there will be no miracle there, only someone wanting to take advantage of your vulnerability.

If you're struggling in your marriage or in a relationship, you have a choice. Either pay someone to tell you what you're doing wrong or ask the one who created relationships in the first place. He's waiting to do the impossible in your life and in your circumstances, if you'll just let Him. He stands at the door and knocks, but you are the only one that can allow Him to come into your life. Death is but for a moment, but eternity is forever.

Losing someone you love is the most difficult thing that some of us will ever have to face. I know, because that week, I faced one of the most crucial times of all. Mom was to me, the epitome of what a mother should be, she was my friend, my sounding board, my biggest fan, my confidant and my gentle persuasion. Her leaving my life left me with a huge void that I wasn't prepared to fill. I couldn't cry because I couldn't accept that it was real, I didn't want to believe it was real, not my mother.

Dad knew how hard I was taking it so when we got back home from the hospital he took me out to the backyard to burn trash like we did when I was a kid. He said,

"We knew that your mother wasn't going to come out of the hospital alive when we put her in there, and so did she. But, she said she didn't want you to know, because she didn't want to take you away from the important ministry that you were doing."

"But dad", I said, "You robbed me of the time I had left with her. I would have spent every spare minute I had at the hospital if I would have known. I loved her dad and I wanted to be with her as she was going through this."

"I'm sorry Michael" he said. "It was her decision and I just went along with it."

I was so angry and hurt and tormented with the fact that I would never see her again in this life. Mom was gone and there was nothing I could do to bring her back. The feeling of desperation just began to overwhelm me. God was this another example of "SHATTERED DREAMS AND BROKEN HEARTS?"

I called my best friend and asked him if he would preach at my mom's funeral and I told my family that I would be at the funeral home later that afternoon to make the needed arrangements. Almost without warning, I started having an extreme headache that I just couldn't get to go away. I called the doctor and he said it was probably from all the stress but if I would come by the hospital he would give me some medication to take care of it. As soon as I got to the hospital, I collapsed. They rushed me in immediately and did a cat scan which revealed that I had a cluster of migraines and the right side of the blood vessels in my head had collapsed. Therefore, it caused me to have a stroke. The only way the doctor could keep me from dying the day after my mother, was to induce a coma through medication.

There I lay, in the hospital, for a week unable to function. Of course I missed my dear mother's funeral and that saddened me very much. My best friend Don, who preached mom's funeral and his family came by to see me in the hospital and saw that I was very sick. I appreciated very much their concern and most of all their prayers. Don's family had always been like a second family to me, especially now in this time of trouble. But, dad and the rest of the family thought that I was making this all up just so I wouldn't have to face mom's funeral. That hurt even more and yet there was nothing that I could have done to control the previous events. The doctor finally called my sister to tell her just how really sick I was. He said, "I don't just induce comas so that someone can escape from reality, your brother had a stroke and he almost died." Well of course they realized then that I really had been sick and they had misjudged me.

Laying in the hospital I gained a lot of understanding for people who lose someone that they love so very much. I had to come to the understanding that in God's eyes, "It's Not The End, It's Just The Beginning."

Death is something
We find hard to understand.
It remains still a mystery
In the Master's Great Plan.

It envelopes our lives
With much sorrow and pain
And often we wonder
Are our lives lived in vain.

But somehow I know
There's a deeper meaning still
Than we can comprehend
About God's perfect will.

All I can say,
Is my trust lies in Him,
Though my lack of understanding
May still remain dim.

Yet there's a warm sense of comfort
A knowing deep inside
That even in death
God's faithfulness still abides.

So weep not, my child
There's a joy that's way past due
What God triumphantly prepared for her
He's preparing also for you.

Copyright 1995 Victoria Lee

***

"Therefore shall a man leave his father and his mother, and shall cleave unto his wife: and they shall be one flesh. Wherefore they are no more twain, but one flesh. What therefore God hath joined together, let not man put asunder."

Matthew 19:5,6

"But if the unbelieving depart, let him depart. A brother or a sister is not under bondage in such cases, but God hath called us to peace.

I Corinthians 7:15
***

Chapter Nine

BROKEN HEARTS

January 15, 1982 Gracelynn gave birth to our second beautiful daughter, Rachel Amber Shaw. She weighed 8 pounds and 11 ounces and she was another wonderful addition to our already out numbered, by females, family. I always knew I would be a family man, someone who enjoyed the strong exuberance that little children could add to your home. These two little girls both knew that they were daddy's little angels and whatever they needed I would try my hardest to provide.

We had already been pastoring Heritage Christian Center for over a year. God had blessed this endeavor in so many ways. Time and time again we saw the Holy Spirit move in our services as if there was a brand new anointing. We never seem to completely learn or know everything there is to know about God and the way He works. We are constantly in the "School of Learning." But, if we will let it be, it can be such a rewarding time to see God mold your life. The changes that can take place inside of you if you are truly open to God's influence, are amazing. The Bible says, "He takes the foolish things of the world to confound the wise." Sometimes the most unlikely person will be the one who God will use to turn a multitude of people toward Him. Who would have thought that a little boy from a broken home, who just wanted to play ball would someday end up traveling all over the country telling people about a God who heals and restores. Even when the times get really rough and I want to give up, God reminds me again the He is still there and He hasn't forgotten that little boy from Decatur, Illinois. You see, God sees us as a finished jewel but all we see is the diamond in the rough. He sees the end even before the beginning. And you don't have to be a preacher for God to use you. He needs everyone of us to be a light, right where we are.

God had already done so much for me that if He never did another thing, I would have to say He had done enough. I was already experiencing things in my own personal life that I never would have imagined and it all came about by believing and searching after His will in my life. He will never push himself on us, but He is so eager to perform things in our lives if we will let Him. I've heard so many people say, "God never speaks to me." And my retort is, "Do you ever speak to Him?" And, if you do, do you ever sit long enough to listen to the answer? A quote I once heard that I love to recall from time to time is,

"God is more, than we can as yet, comprehend, that He is."

I think that's so beautiful, don't try to figure out how big God is, just know that He is and that He is a rewarder of those who diligently seek

Him. Nothing, nothing, nothing in life will fulfill you more than a relationship with the creator of your very body, soul and spirit. I don't mean do you know about Him, but do you "KNOW HIM". I challenge you to spend some time letting the Lord reveal himself to you and you'll find that the happiest years are still ahead.

***

There are always ups and downs in ministry and pastoring a church certainly doesn't make you exempt from either. Sometimes the pastor and his wife are meant to be the heroes of all heroes. Able to leap over the tallest buildings in a single bound. But excuse me, wasn't that meant for "Superman". Oddly enough though people just seem to expect more than you can possibly give. Gracelynn and I found ourselves giving until the spigot just ran dry and we had to desperately find a way to re-fill the reservoir.

In the ministry you find it very hard to find friends that you can really count on. Friends that aren't trying to suck the life out of you. Friends that you can depend on through thick and thin. Sometimes people expect you to be almost like God and they place you on a pedestal never realizing that if you fall, that they will fall with you. Then if you fail to measure up to what their expectation of God is, you become a failure to them. We as ministers never volunteered to be Gods, only representatives to show you the way to Almighty God. But nevertheless, we sometimes get caught in the crossfire whether we choose to or not. And so it was with Gracelynn and I, we had eventually pastored the church for four years, had been to PTL ministering several times and thought things couldn't get any better. Then, we had a major church split. Anytime something like that happens, you question everything and everyone around you. It's like all of a sudden you wonder who your friends really are or if you even have or had any to begin with. You think how could someone I trusted betray me like this. And the noose seems to get tighter and tighter.

Well even in the best of marriages there comes a breaking point and Gracelynn had reached hers. She had been through all of the ups and downs that she felt she could handle in this lifetime. She was tired of trying to be everything to everybody and not ever being able to just relax and be who she was. She was hurt and wounded and felt like she would never be able to recover if she remained being married to me and the ministry. To her it meant you have to give up everything you have and everything you are just to survive. She had been through all the "SHATTERED DREAMS AND BROKEN HEARTS" that she could stand. To her being in the ministry meant trial after trial after trial and she was ready to get off of the proverbial witness stand.

One of the most difficult things in the world that a minister or a man could possibly ever hear is when his wife says, "I want a divorce." Suddenly I was faced with a problem that I didn't know how to handle. I had often counseled many couples in the past and helped them to overcome their problems, but now I was caught in the same situation and I didn't have the power to stop it. I couldn't really blame Gracelynn for the way she felt, because in so many ways it was justified. I knew that God hadn't taken his hand off of me but to Gracelynn, she had gotten to the point that all she could see was the problems and not the solutions. She saw people hurt and let down by the ministry and by myself. She also saw that the ministry demands a great deal from you and so many ministers put their ministries before their families and then they fail in both areas. God has never meant for that to happen. So many of us allow ourselves to get to that point, I know it's very easy to do and quite understandable. What was sad though, is God was still in control but we just didn't know it. Or should I say, we lacked "God Confidence."

For the first time in over thirteen years, I was now all alone and facing more of my dreams that had been shattered and a heart that had been broken in two. Yet, I still believed that God wasn't finished with me.

One of the most controversial subjects in the church is in the area of divorce. It seems that a divorced person is less acceptable in the pulpit than murderers, rapists and drug dealers or other individuals who have committed other crimes. There is such a double set of standards. If a man says I spent ten years in the penitentiary and then met the Lord and was

"Born Again" and God has called me to preach, then we all would shout for joy and open our arms wide to accept him. But if a man struggles through life as a Christian who has always tried to live with high moral standards and then gets a divorce, the chances of even being accepted as a deacon or minister in the church is questionable.

For years there has only been one grounds for divorce that was acceptable for the church and that is the area of adultery. Yet it's time for us all to read the rest of the scriptures.

I Corinthians 7:15 - But if the unbelieving depart, let him depart. A brother or sister is not under bondage in such cases: but God hath called us to peace.

Here Paul states emphatically, that there is another grounds scripturally for divorce, that is in the area of "Unbelief". I do not condone divorce, but I've had to live through it and deal with it personally and with the Lord.

A believer can also become a "dis-believer" and turn from God, even to a reprobate mind. In which case, Paul states we are not under bondage (law of Moses), but God has called us to peace (which means) "New Beginnings". Just like in II Corinthians 5:17, we through forgiveness become "New Creations" and old sin is passed away.

If there was no truth to this, then David and many others in the Bible would be in hell, darkness and torment, because in God's eyes there is no difference between white lies, murder, adultery, or divorce, they are all sin!!! If David was forgiven and restored and his sins were "supposedly greater" than the sins of the major ministries who recently fell or someone who has gone through divorce, then why are their trials or problems or even sins, not forgiven as well by man, as they are by God!!!

We can no longer stick our heads in the sand and try to abide by man made laws and constitutions that made divorced people second class citizens. DIVORCE is not the unpardonable sin. The enemy has attacked the church with every weapon at his disposal and more ministries are being destroyed because people don't expect their ministers to make mistakes or ever fail in life. I think sometimes if they would spend as much time seeking their own relationship with God as they do putting their minister in an exalted position, then they would understand failure much easier. Man will always fail you, because he is man. Set your eyes on Jesus, the Author and Finisher of your faith. But, it's so much easier to look to the man, to let him give you all the answers. That way you don't have to do the seeking yourself, you don't have to spend the time in God's presence to get the needed answers because you go to the preacher for the answers. And then, one day you wake up and the man you chose to follow makes a mistake similar to the many that you have made so many times before. But his is inexcusable in your eyes and sometimes we even blame God for how the man failed to be what we had called him to be. Do you know how many people have stayed in abusive relationships simply because the church frowned on them for dissolving the relationship. Rather than disappoint the self-appointed prophets, they stay in the abusive relationship that is no good for them or for the furtherance of the Kingdom of God.

We've got to remember that all of us are susceptible to the attacks of the enemy. None of us are exempt. We all fall short of the glory of God. But when we do, we must pick ourselves up, dust ourselves off and start all over again, without condemnation from the world around us. We all deserve the chance to be everything that God has called us to be. And, we can only get there if we allow ourselves to not be pulled down by other men's' expectations of us. The bottom line is "God can turn it around for us". He can work everything out for our good if we will just let Him.

So on June 5, 1985 Gracelynn and I ended our 13 and a half year marriage. We had been through a lot of trials, some that were worse than others. And, we had experienced some terrific triumphs that would leave lasting memories. Along with all of that, we shared two beautiful children that were to remain the most important part of our lives. So even in the midst of what seemed like defeat, we did have a lot to rejoice in but it took us a while to realize that. Often in the midst of our pain we don't even remember the good times we once shared. We have a tendency to focus on all the defeats instead of the victories and it just drags us farther and farther down. I wish I could say that Gracelynn and I both popped right back in shape instantly, but that just wouldn't be true. We were both wounded and we needed time to heal. Only God knew what direction that we were both headed in now and we just had to be willing to follow.

It wasn't easy continuing in the ministry as a divorced man. Since people are so gripped by traditions, they very often are unable to see that you are still the same person, you are just wearing different apparel. I know that being divorced doesn't change the anointing that God has on a preacher anymore than it changes a person's love for God if they are a smoker or gossiper or if they have a bad temper etc. Being divorced means we've felt pain and we've experienced failure. But who hasn't felt pain and who hasn't experienced failure?

I'm reminded of an incident when I was ministering in California in another man's church, as a divorced man. We were in our second week of the meetings and the Presbyter of the Assemblies of God for that district came to evaluate the church. When he found out that I was preaching even though I was divorced, he ordered the pastor of the church to shut the meetings down. But, the pastor refused to do it because God was doing wonderful things during the services and he realized that the Presbyter really didn't understand the circumstances.

The Presbyter of course pursued the issue without seemingly any compassion toward me and the pastor said,

"Look, when this meeting is over you can have my credentials if you want them but I'm not ending these services until God ends them. I know that Brother Mike was sent here for us and I want him to continue."

You probably could hear the shouts of joy that were raging in my heart. I was so in awe that God had come to my rescue through this pastor.

After the meetings had come to an end there happened to be a local meeting in town to vote on a new Presbyter. It was rumored that this man would probably be re-elected and the pastor thought it would be good for me to come along and see what happens. At first I said, "I don't think that's a very good idea since the man doesn't even like me." But the pastor insisted, saying that he felt like that was what God had told him. So I agreed and accompanied the pastor to the meeting. To our astonishment the Presbyter who had been so aggressive toward me, stood up and with tears in his eyes began to explain that the night before, his wife of 34 years left him a note and ran out on him. As it turns out, she had just gotten "burned out" from the ministry and was tired and hurt and just unwilling to go any further. Here was a man who had put others down for years because of divorce and now, he was reaping what he had sown. He was terribly upset and discouraged about the whole incident and of course extremely embarrassed because he had talked against divorce for so long. I waited for other ministers to go over to him and encourage or console him but no one ever did. Finally, I went to him and whispered in his ear and said,

"Brother I've been there and I know how you feel."

He looked at me, swallowed hard and said, "I know."

Of course they didn't re-elect him as the Presbyter which oversees all the churches in that district. He ended up resigning the church and leaving feeling like his life of ministry was over. Isn't that ironic, his wife left because she didn't want to be in the ministry and that caused him to end up leaving anyway. I tried to encourage him that his ministry wasn't over and that God still wanted to use him. It's so hard when the people you have spent your life ministering for and with see you as unworthy because of hurtful occurrences that you have no control over. But God doesn't want you to give up, he wants you to stand and watch Him perform restoration in your life. Remember, "He is more, than we can as yet, comprehend, that He is."

***

"Jesus answered, do you now believe?

Behold the hour cometh,

that ye shall be scattered,

every man to his own, and shall leave

me alone, and yet (I am not alone)

because the Father is with me.

These things I have spoken unto you,

that in me ye might have peace.

In the world you shall have

tribulation, but be of good cheer;

for I have overcome the world.

John 16:31-33

***

Chapter Ten

DARKEST, JUST BEFORE THE DAWN

Being single was not easy for me, especially since I was a preacher. It's really like you're living in a glass house and everybody is watching you. Believe me preachers have the same kind of needs and desires as any man alive. After all, God did make Eve because He said, "It's not good for man to be alone." When you spend a lot of time in the word, the love that God gives you for people naturally causes you to yearn for a special person that you can share that love with. But, the whole world is waiting for you the "preacher" to mess up so they can condemn you. If you were just "Joe Blow" and you needed a mate, everybody would rally around you and say, "Go for it." But preachers have to be measured and analyzed and ridiculed and judged about every situation or relationship.

At one point, I found myself engaged to a young lady who had a small child. I was eager and excited about preparing a future for us but her parents sadly enough were not. Then I made a mistake that I didn't realize was a mistake at the time but everyone around me supposedly did. You know it's amazing how people expect so much out of you. I am not Jesus, I am not God the Father, nor am I the

Holy Spirit. Like I said before, I'm just a man called of God to lead others into His presence. I'm flesh and human and sometimes carnal just like anyone else reading this book.

So, I began dating a divorced woman out of the church. I thought that her relationship with her ex-husband was totally over but I came to find out that it wasn't. As it turns out the husband came back into her life and wanted to make mine a living hell. He proceeded to go to one of the deacons and express his grievances about his lack of confidence in my integrity. I guess the only way to assure himself that he could win his wife back, was by humiliating me. I was threatened by a lawsuit which they assumed I would not fight in order to keep my name from being damaged. Because of the tremendous amount of slander that was told to the deacon, I was confronted by him to resign the church. I'm telling you, I felt like a brick wall had just caved in on me.

It seemed like no matter how devoted I was or how sincere, someone was always ready and willing to destroy me. I had already lost my wife, lost other things that the Lord had given me and now this man was trying to take my good name as well. Ashamedly I went home one night after the beginning of this ordeal and again said, "Lord I just can't take it anymore." You know the enemy of our soul loves to hear us say that. He loves to get us to the point when we are ready to give up. If he can, then he knows that we will never fulfill the magnitude of victories that God has in store for us. We will never be all that we can be and we'll just be a statistic of all the people that failed to reach God's best. Because you see the word says, "We wrestle not against flesh and blood but against principalities and powers and the rulers of darkness." But God said we can be overcomers. He will take what the enemy meant for bad and turn it around for our good. Did you know that He can take every circumstance that comes into your life and build strength in you, if you'll let Him. Keep your eyes on Him, the Author and Finisher of your faith. It's so hard for us to see the whole picture like God sees it. If we could just learn to trust Him even in what seems to be our defeats. God loves you, like you've never known love before. Learn to say, "O.K. God turn this around for my good. Let me see it like you see it, because I'm going to trust you. Everything I am or will be, I owe to you. What do you want me to do or be for you God."

As I said earlier, I went home that night feeling like all hope had left my life. Sitting there in the dark, I started thinking about how my wife had left me and I was 2000 miles away from my children. I felt so alone and unable to see any real reason to go on. My life had seen some victories but oh how the defeats outweighed them. I was in so much pain that I just wanted to close my eyes and tell the world good-bye. I began to reflect back over the years and all the things that I had been through. The accident, my divorce and all the rumors and slanderous words. Then I thought about all the good things that I had accomplished. I remembered all the people that I had a chance to minister to and how many thousands of people were saved and healed and baptized in the Holy Ghost. I began to reflect on the times that I had pastored and tried to help so many people who were young and old. It seemed like a hundred things were going through my mind as I sat on the floor staring at the pictures of my two little girls and crying with such a sense of hopelessness.

The darkness seemed to make it easier when I eventually made my decision to end my life. When we get to that point, like I know many of us have, we convince ourselves that no one really cares one way or the other. We imagine all kinds of negative feelings about our worth on this earth and our purpose for living. We know that no one plans on getting to this stage but it's the plan that the enemy had all along. If he can get you to focus on yourself and your own problems rather than the needs of others, then he's made a gigantic step in the destruction of your life, or marriage or relationship or anything else you find yourself having difficulties with.

We live in a generation in which many people are coming to a place where they feel like there are no answers and no way out or at least, that's what the enemy wants them to think. Many have discovered that all the money in the world can't buy them happiness and joy and peace in their life. Only by knowing Jesus can you have real peace. I'm not talking about religion or following a particular pastor that you have put up on a pedestal. I'm talking about a relationship with the true and living God. The problem is, some of us don't believe that, "He is the rewarder of those that diligently seek Him." The world is on a fast pace and seems to be spinning faster and faster like an amusement park ride. Many are not sure how to stop the ride and get off. It's easier to just jump off and get rid of their fears and doubts in life through drugs and alcohol. Or they get their future read by astrologers who seem to have all the answers, they think. Americans are spending millions on these solutions, but to no avail, because the problems will still be there tomorrow, even though the supposed fix may be there for today.

Many people are facing the darkest periods of their life and it seems like there is no light to chase away the darkness. Yet the Bible says that we as Christians are the light to this dark world. But, how many people really see that to be true? When people are hurting if all they've seen is religious bondage, then the last thing in the world they want is to bind themselves up with the ritual. But if they see a true and living God that wants to comfort them and make them whole, then they will come running. The Bible says, "The goodness of the Lord leads a man to repentance." If you've ever truly experienced God's forgiving and loving nature, then you'll always run to Him when you're hurting and in need. Step under the spout where the glory pours out, and let Him show you the way.

Sitting there in that dark room, I couldn't help but feel empty inside. It seemed like all of my strength and all of my abilities to handle every situation had been depleted from me. I felt scared and worried but most of all, I felt alone. I suddenly realized the feelings that my step-sister had experienced the day that we talked for the last time on the phone a few years back. She said,

"Michael, I need someone to talk to about problems that I'm facing in my life, my home and my marriage. Can you come and see me and maybe we could talk for a while?"

I remember looking at my watch and schedule as she was speaking and thinking to myself; "I'm pretty busy."

"Sandy maybe I can come in a couple of weeks, when I finish the meeting that I am in right now, if that's alright with you?"

There was a quietness on the other end of the phone and I thought that she was thinking about what I had said and then she softly said,

"That will be fine, I guess."

Then as quickly as the conversation started, it ended and I was hanging up the phone, knowing in my heart that something was wrong. But, I did nothing except say a quick prayer, thinking that was all that she needed from me at the time. We need to always be ready when the Lord brings someone to us that we can comfort or help in their time of need. Sandy was crying out for help and yet the man of God that she counted on to help her, let her down. It wasn't until later, that I was told by the family that Sandy had obviously gotten off of the phone and gone into the bathroom and hung herself. As I sat there crying my heart out I realized that I could have helped her and I chose not to at that moment, because it didn't fit into my schedule.

People please listen to the leading of the Holy Spirit in your life. It can cause changes to happen that you never knew were possible. Maybe you have never felt that loneliness that can come upon you and steal away your faith, joy and peace that you have depended on for so long. Maybe you have been comfortable in your life and really believed that nothing would ever happen to you. If that's so, then I'm happy for you but watch out the Bible says, "The enemy is like a roaring lion, seeking whom he may devour." We need to be instant in season and out. In other words, be ready for God to use you to help someone else even if it inconveniences you.

Even Jesus on the day He went to the garden to pray asked his friends to stay awake and pray with him, yet they chose to fall asleep. They were just too tired to tarry. They were too caught up in their own problems, to take on the problems of the world.

Listen to the words of Jesus, as they are recorded in the Gospels and listen to the loneliness that He felt when He thought that no one cared.

Matthew 26:36-45 - "Then came Jesus with them unto a place called Gethsemane, and said unto the disciples, Sit ye here, while I go and pray.

And He took with Him Peter and the two sons of Zebedee, and began to be sorrowful and very heavy.

Then said he unto them, "My soul is exceedingly sorrowful even unto death: tarry ye here, and watch with me."
And he went a little further, and fell on his face, and prayed, saying, O my Father, if it be possible, let this cup pass from me but nevertheless not as I will, but as thou will.

And he came unto the disciples, and findeth them asleep, and said unto them and Peter; "What, could you not watch with me just one hour? Watch and pray, that ye enter not into temptation; (the Spirit is indeed willing, but the flesh is weak)."

During the most difficult times, the Lord asked those that He had chosen to stay awake with him and pray. Like many people then and now, they were just too tired. It had been a hard day and they needed their rest and besides that, they figured the Lord would understand. How many times have we done just the opposite of what the Lord wanted us to do in our life. Surely He would understand, that all this traveling and all of the things that we had done the previous day, would drain us and cause us to want to sleep. Besides, there will be plenty of time to pray and plenty of time to get the work done that the Lord has for us.

Here was a time in the life of the Lord, in which we could see his human weaknesses crying out and looking for a way out of the problems that He was facing. Surely God would listen to His Son and spare Him from the agony and the pain that was coming! Yet Jesus was alone and heard nothing. Heaven was silent and the angels were quiet to the words of the Son. Angels wanted to respond to the cry of the Savior, but they must obey. The prayers of the Savior seemed to bounce off of Heaven, as He knelt there all alone and the cry of his heart seemed to fall on deaf ears. He was alone at the most difficult time of his life and even those that were close to Him didn't seem to care.

There would be those that would say, "yes, but that was the Lord and He had to face it alone." He faced it alone, so that we might know that He knows exactly how we feel at each and every moment. At the cross Jesus was alone and He cried.

Matthew 27:46 - "And about the ninth hour, Jesus cried with a loud voice, saying "Eli, Eli, lama sa Bach tha ni", which means, "My God, My God, why hast thou forsaken me?"

Loneliness is one of the greatest tools of the enemy and one of the most difficult things in life to face. Loneliness when it comes, is like the darkness that sweeps in at dusk, ready to encompass the remaining light and sweep us into an everlasting night. I am reminded of the saying that goes like this, "It is always the darkest, just before the dawn." You may be facing the greatest darkness in your life and you may think that there is no other recourse except to just end it all. I know, because as I sat on that floor that evening that's all that I could think about.

With a bottle of sleeping pills in one hand and a glass of water in the other, I thought I'll just make it easier for everyone including God. This way I would never be able to disappoint anyone again and I'd be free of the guilt of letting God down one more time. Yet what I didn't know, was that the Lord was listening and waiting to show me that He still cared about me and about the problems that I was having in life.

Just as I was about to take the lid off of the pills, the phone rang. I had no intention of picking up that phone so it just rang and rang and kept on ringing. I remember sitting there thinking why don't they just hang up so I can get on with this. Finally, I got so irritated that I just jerked up the receiver and said, "Hello". On the other end of the line was my two little daughters Carrieann who was eight and Rachel who was three at the time. They said,

"Daddy what's wrong."

I tried to pretend that nothing was the matter but Carrieann just wouldn't buy that. She said,

"Daddy, you always told us to listen to the Lord's voice, and as we were watching T.V., we suddenly looked at each other and said, There's something wrong with Daddy, we've got to call him."

Inside I was thinking, "God just somehow get them off of this phone so I can go ahead and end my misery." Then I heard my little Rachel say,

"Daddy please don't do it, we love you."

After hearing the sound of their little pleading voices, I realized that nothing was more important to me than them. I knew that in spite of how I felt about myself, those little girls needed me. I had promised God when I went through my divorce that they would never suffer or have a need for anything. I said if they were ever in trouble and needed me that I would be there. Well now, I realized that they were in trouble. They were about to loose part of the security of a father that every child so desperately needs. I reached up quickly and flipped on the light switch and it was as if death left the room. At that moment I thought, God I can't quit. It looks like my life is never going to be without incidents of failure but you anticipated this, you knew it before it ever happened and you can turn it around for my good.

Hanging up the phone, I began to praise God and thank Him for His mercy and love. Within a few minutes, there was a knock at the door and several of the families from the church were standing there to tell me they loved me and didn't want me to leave the congregation. Yet, I knew my time there was over and it was time to move on to bigger and better things in the Lord.

There will be times of loneliness and times of despair. There will be times when you want to throw up your hands and say, "I quit." But you must remember that God is not through with you yet, and that He has greater things for you to do with your life. He has greater things that He wants you to do for people and one day the things that you have gone through and conquered, will help someone else. You will be there to tell them how God brought you through the trials and tribulations of your own life.

Don't let people or circumstances rob you of the greatest thing that God could ever give you and that is your life. I know what it's like to lose friends and even loved ones to this disease of the mind that says you can't go on. But I'm here to tell you that you can go on and that life is worth living for tomorrow. If you have made a quality decision to allow Jesus to be Lord of your life, then every problem that you have is His problem also. I promise you, if you will let go, and let God - He will turn that circumstance around. Because, He is always there. And, the darkest hour comes just before the dawn.

After being single for about six years and living in the town of Clinton,, Iowa I received an invitation to go to a small church. I went for what I thought was a one day meeting and ended up staying twelve weeks. To my astonishment, I met my present beautiful wife, Rosemary. I guess it was almost like love at first sight. We had so much that we wanted to share together. It was a chance to recapture the feeling of being in love that we had somehow both lost along the way. It was a real time of refreshing for both of us. The minute I met her the first thing that attracted me to her was her bright eyes and warm smile. I knew that God didn't want me to be alone because that way I never could feel totally complete.

Many times I had prayed that God would give me a wife that was beautiful as well as understanding. He gave me far above what I ever thought or asked for. I wanted someone who was wise and yet not in the ministry, someone who would just be there for me. I wanted a prayer warrior that would hold me up as I went into the battlefield of life. Rosemary is all of that and more. She's someone that you can trust and rely on to always be there for you. She really is my best friend and an asset in my life. When we got married she had three children and I had two, so we felt like we knew what the "Brady Bunch" family must have been like. Her children have become my children and I love them as if they were my own flesh and blood. So life began again in a new way with a new start and many roads to travel. A new dawn, at least for a season, had finally arrived.

***

"The Lord is my rock

and my fortress,

and my deliverer;

my God,

my strength,

in whom I will trust;

my buckler, and the horn

of my salvation,

and my high tower.

Psalm 18:2

***

Chapter Eleven

VICTORY PREVAILS

Staring at the reflection in the window, I could hardly recognize the individual that was staring back at me. I thought I had known this person and yet he seemed different. Gone was the joy and happiness that had been a part of my life and expressions which had touched the lives of millions of people through the years. Lives that had been changed through television, radio or crusades. Gone was the strong bass and baritone voice that had sung to millions and ministered the Word of God. Gone was the special anointing that had been given by the Holy Spirit and had touched people from all backgrounds.

For the moment there were dry lips and a rasping voice plus swollen eyes that reflected hours of crying. Along with it was a face that showed fear where strength, courage and faith had once been. The mirror reflected a dejected and lonely person that felt like the world was closing in and that all hope had been removed.

The only sounds to be heard were the clanging shut of doors in the distance and the voices of people with no names. People who were now crying out in fear and hurt and loneliness like the individual in the mirror, but only their voices could be heard. These were the same people who just hours earlier had come to this place and believed that a friend or family member would soon come and help them in their time of need. This was a place of loneliness and hurt and pain where no one seemed to care or even listen.

Their voices were now filled with cursing and crying and pleading and screaming. There were those that begged and held out hope that someone would come and help take them from this place of captivity. Yet there was silence except for those who could move freely throughout the facility. Even those individuals walked in silence, immune to what was being said and even asked for, from those that were bound. Their response would be one of promises but ones never kept.

This was a place where everyone is guilty until proven innocent and where individual freedoms are suddenly taken with the sound of the closing of the doors. It is a lonely place where many can look into the mirrors that stand before them and reflect on their lives. They see the hurt and the pain that they have caused others but most of all have caused upon themselves. It is a time of reflection but it is also a time for examination.

Standing in front of that mirror of captivity I began to realize that I was a very lonely person and that the serious charges which had been filed against me the previous day were very real. For three years I had not realized what had taken place nor did I know about the charges that had been filed against me during that time. I had moved out of the state and unknowingly had left some returned checks behind. I was told by my lawyer that charges had been filed the week after when they could not locate me, even though a forwarding address had been left at the time.

I cannot express the embarrassment that I felt and shame that I caused the Lord and the ministry and those that I loved by being placed in this situation. Yet it was a problem that I had to deal with and it needed to be resolved before taking any further steps in the ministry.

I realized then that this wasn't something that just happened, but like a terrible disease or a "sin which so easily besets us" according to

Hebrews 12:1,2 -

Wherefore seeing we also are compassed about with so great a cloud of witnesses, let us lay aside every weight, and the sin which doth so easily beset us, and let us run with patience the race that is set before us.

Looking unto Jesus the author and finisher of our faith; who for the joy that was set before him endured the cross, despising the shame, and is set down at the right hand of the throne of God.

It needed to be dealt with and now the Lord was placing me in a place where I had to deal with my sin, just like David did, when confronted by Nathan the prophet in II Samuel the 12th Chapter.

Like my mom used to say, "Sometimes we are too close to the forest to see the trees." Many Christians don't want to admit that there is sin in their life, for they really believe that they have overcome their sin or problems through forgiveness in Christ. It's true, Jesus does forgive us when we accept Him into our lives, but very often we still need our minds renewed in certain areas. Our thoughts need to be changed in order to live victorious lives. Remember the Bible says, "His thoughts are not always our thoughts." I guarantee you the only way you can have His thoughts, is by having His Spirit flow through you and His word envelope you. Sin in many peoples lives, is like cutting the grass that is filled with weeds. You may cut away the appearance of the weed, but it's still there as long as there is a root. Until the root is pulled, the problem whether it's a weed or sin will rise up again and again in a person's life until it is dealt with.

That is where the area of **RESTORATION** and the theme and message of this book begins to work and take over in the life of an individual. Webster's dictionary defines Restoration as bringing back to a former position or condition. To renew, rebuild or bring back to the original state.

Remember, "Without Restoration, there is no Deliverance". And "Without Deliverance there is no Victory over Sin".

But, how does that really work?

Without the renewing of your mind concerning a particular problem area, there can be no deliverance(freedom from the problem.)

And if there is no freedom from the problem there can be no victory (overcoming the enemy or becoming successful in your struggle.)

You never stop being a thief until you have renewed your mind about the destructiveness of your actions. Then you can be free to feel the conviction of the Lord who will then cause you to be successful with your struggle over the enemy.

How do you renew your mind? By feeding the Word of God into your life.

"We've all failed, but Jesus never fails, and His word will cleanse you completely."

The Lord is a righteous judge and when He looks at us through His son Jesus Christ after forgiveness, then it doesn't matter what the accuser might say, because we become free from all condemnation and our sins are forgiven, even though at times there may still be some repercussions from the former deeds that we've done. The law of reaping and sowing is still in effect. If you robbed a bank, you may still have to go to jail even though you have repented of your sins and asked Jesus into your life. If you have abused your body with a variety of drugs for years, you may still have the debilitating effects throughout your body. But the good news is, Jesus can turn it all around. He will either deliver you from any effects, or He will use them(the scars of your past) as a means of Restoration in your own life, as well as others.

In my own life, I realized that where I was, I could do nothing about it, and that is where the Lord's work in each of us must begin.

First, I was facing extradition, when the Lord through the Holy Spirit showed me that I could fight it and be released upon a hearing before the court. The next day, even after so called minister friends told me that I would not be released and all hope seemed to vanish, I went before the judge and was placed on the lowest amount of bond that could be set. I was now free to fight the extradition and at the same time to find out how these events had taken place.

Second, I was able to have a hearing before the most honorable and respected judge in the area, where my mistakes and crime had been committed, in which I showed receipts and many letters and statements that proved eventual payment on all of the checks. However, I still accepted my guilt to the charges and was placed on probation which ended after 6 months. Can you even begin to imagine what it felt like knowing that I was guilty and had made mistakes, but God in all of His mercy was letting me know, that I was forgiven and that He was still in control of my life and the affairs of men. Thank God, He doesn't hold our stupidity against us. We can get so caught up in the busyness of life sometimes that we have a tendency to hang ourselves. But if our hearts are right, God will see us through. I had just faced another "Broken Heart", but God immediately put me on the mend.

It is during this time, that you learn about people and discover who your friends and loved ones really are. It is here that you learn whether or not people are going to stand by you or whether they will turn and run during the most difficult times of your life.

Many people are good and loyal friends as long as things are going good. But let the difficult times come and you will discover and learn about those that you can depend upon and trust in life. Like marriage, commitment should be for a lifetime in spite of the weather and in spite of the problems that we might have to face.

The same is true in our Christian walk and the responsibilities that we have in this life for each other and to ourselves. We must remember that we have a responsibility that lies deeper than just for ourselves and our families. We have a responsibility to others that the Lord has put into our lives.

We live in a generation in which many ministers, leaders and even lay people are failing to reach out to other people. Then we wonder why our churches are struggling and why people are not flocking to our services. We wonder why people are having a hard time believing what we are saying, because we fail to live the kind of life that reflects that of the Lord Jesus Christ. And that's not with condemnation, retaliation or judgement, but with the love and compassion and understanding that is also given to us by the Lord. We must remember that the church is a reflection of the ministry and not always of the Lord. Some people have spent their whole life being in subjection to a man when in fact it wasn't what God had intended at all. Preacher whether you like it or not, the people that attend your church will often become a reflection of you and your teachings and the way you conduct your life. So, be careful because you will be held accountable for how you treated God's children.

Sometimes it seems that ministers are spending more time building their own kingdoms and trying to control people that God sends their way. We need to remind ourselves that the church we pastor and the people that God has given us charge over, belong to the Lord and not to us. We are only to lead by example but never to control.

One of the greatest areas where ministers fail is by their example that they establish before the Body of Christ. We have a favorite saying or excuse I call it, that we use quite often when we don't want to do something; "I'll Pray About It." I have often asked myself and others across this nation in our crusades, why should we pray about something that the Lord has already instructed us to do in His word? The answer seems simple, "We don't want to do it!" Many of us are guilty of this response in our own lives and in the way we respond to others. We are afraid to be involved when it comes to other people's problems.

Preachers are afraid that their reputations will be marred by association with those that have failed in their calling to the Lord. They become afraid that their own reputation in the area will be tarnished by some scandal or by reaching out and helping those that have made mistakes. The excuse is often given, "You made your bed, now sleep in it."

For too long we have taught in our seminaries and we have passed along in our ministries the idea that preachers are to be loners and not have anything to do with the Body of Christ. We get mad when visiting ministers make friends with the members of our congregation, because they are our people and we become so afraid that they might give money to their ministry, instead of our church or maybe to us. We have a saying for this, that I learned a long time ago, and that is Hogwash! There is no where in scripture that states or backs these reasons for the fear that preachers have in the ministry. Many of our fears are created from our own insecurities and from our own doubts and fears.

We have a responsibility to inform the world. Also to show, those that God has given us charge over, the reflection of the Word of God and the life of Jesus Christ our Lord and Savior! In the scriptures, we have an example that our Lord has given us through the writings of Paul which are found in,

Galations 6:1-2: "Brethren, if a man be overtaken in a fault, ye which are spiritual, restore such as one in the spirit of meekness; considering thyself, lest thou also be tempted. Bear ye one another's burdens, and so fulfill the law of Christ!"

Now I want to share the same passage of scriptures only from a Living Bible translation. "If you see your brother stumble, go to him without question, restoring him to where he was, because the next time it may be you that falls and who will be there to pick you up when you fall down. Share in each other's troubles and problems, and so obey our Lord's command."

Maybe our eye's should be open to what God's word is saying to each of us, especially those in the ministry. It is a command and not a choice that we have to minister and restore people. We must be willing to help them and even bail them out during their time of need.

There is coming a day when we will need each other more than ever before and if we cannot count on each other now, how will we be able to depend on each other when times become more difficult in life. It should be a joy and a privilege to help someone in need! It should be exciting that the Lord has chosen us to be the example at that moment in time, in which He has brought people into our lives and into our churches. "Let us do for others what He would do for us in the same situation and let us be reminded that one day it could be us in the same situation."

Maybe we should be reminded of those times as children when we went to the amusement park or carnival and entered into the House of Mirrors. Standing in front of the mirror we saw a reflection that had been distorted by the reflection in the mirror. Instead of seeing the person that we had always known, we saw an individual that was distorted and ugly and whose figure was marred by what appeared to be peculiarities that would make you different from everyone else in life.

Our first reaction was one of laughter, but what if the person we were looking at really looked that way. What would be our response and how would we treat them and respond to their needs. The old saying still abounds even today, "Don't judge a book by its cover!" The image in the mirror could be each of us without the grace and the mercy of God in our lives. We can never change the outward appearance without an operation, but we can change the inward image that has an affect on what the outward appearance will be in life.

The outward appearance of a person does not reflect what may be on the inside. There are many good looking and beautiful people in the world, but they may have a negative and distorted image inside that would make them ugly and hideous to those around them. The same is true in the ministry and in the church. Therefore, we should frequently ask ourselves are we really reflecting Jesus Christ or are we spending more time trying to be something that we are not. As preachers we can preach good messages, but if we fail to be an example of what the church is all about and what Christ means to us, then our preaching and our testimony are in vain.

There is an answer and it comes from the transformation, that Christ brings into each of our lives, beginning on the inside and reflecting on the outside when we look in the mirror each day.

***

"And these three men: Shadrach, Meshach and Abednego
fell down bound into the midst of the burning
fiery furnace. Then Nebuchadnezzar, the King was
astonished, and rose up in haste, and spake, and
said unto his counselors, did we not cast three men
bound into the fire? And they said unto the King,

True O King

He answered and said, Lo, I see four men loose walking
in the midst of fire, and they are not hurt; and the form
of the fourth is like unto the son of God and then
Nebuchadnezzar came near to the mouth of the burning
fiery furnace and spoke unto
Shadrach, Meshach, and Abednego, saying ye
servants of the most high God, come forth and they
came out of the fire. And the princes, governors and
captains, and the Kings counselors being gathered
together, saw these men, upon whose bodies the fire
had no power, nor was a hair of their head singed,
neither were their coats changed, nor the smell of fire
had passed on them..

Daniel 3:23-27

***

Chapter Twelve

LET THE REDEEMED OF THE LORD, SAY SO

When was the last time that you were so far down, that you wondered if you would be able to look up? Everyday we go through problems and situations in life that seem to drag us under like a current or undertow in the water, that we are swimming in called life.

I remember as a child swimming with my family at my grandparents cottage on the lake in Indiana. My dad had pointed out to me before going into the water, certain areas that would be difficult to swim in. Needless to say, I must have missed one of those areas, because no sooner had dad dived into the water and started swimming out away from the shore, than I found myself trying to follow after him. Having waded into the water about fifteen feet I suddenly dropped out of sight and was sinking fast because I couldn't keep my head above the water.

Realizing that I was in trouble, my father came and reached down his hands and grabbed me and lifted me out of the hole that I had slipped into and placed me on a spot where I could once again stand up. Without my father there to save me that day, it would have been very easy to have died at a very early age. I wonder how many times, our Heavenly Father has had to save each of us from those times that we slipped and fell off of the solid ground that we were standing on in life.

How many times have you cried out to Him when you were hurting and longing for someone to talk to and yet all you heard was silence. It was like the moments before a storm in which the wind will seem to stop and nothing seems to move and suddenly the skies grow dark and the winds begin to blow and the waves seem to rise until we can't see the bright sun that is still shining above the storm.

Foundations are important to the walk of the believer and without a solid foundation, we are going to face many more problems in this life.

Matthew 7:24-27 says, "Therefore whosoever heareth these sayings of mine, and doeth them, I will liken him unto a wise man, which built his house upon a rock. And the rain descended and the floods came, and the winds blew and beat upon the house and it fell not, for it was built upon a rock.

And everyone that heareth these sayings of mine, and doeth them not, shall be likened unto a foolish man, which built his house on the sand. And the rain descended and the flood came, and the winds blew and beat upon that house; and it fell, and great was the fall of it."

Many people's lives and hopes have been shattered because the foundation that they were living upon or standing upon was not strong. Too many people have a foundation that is built on wood and hay and stubble. Theirs is a foundation that cannot stand in the midst of the storm. They have been too busy seeking short term successes that they believed would allow them to sit back and live on easy street. However, had they devoted more time in establishing a sound foundation then they would be far better prepared to withstand any major storm that might occur.

Don't get me wrong, there is nothing wrong with working hard, saving and preparing for our families. But for many people they are so caught up in their own world that they don't have time to stop and smell the roses. People really believe that their security is in their ability to prepare for the future. They will spend thousands of dollars on insurance and on stocks and IRA's and savings for the future, yet they won't prepare themselves or their loved ones for eternity.

Many Christians are the same way, they will spend more time involved in the things of the world, than they will in the things of God. They are "Sunday Only Christians" who give God their time and their money for one day, believing that they have done His will. Yet when they are in trouble and need a quick fix or a deliverance from their situations, then they will devote extra time and effort calling out to God. When He delivers them out of their problems, they immediately return to where they were at before they were inconvenienced by their trials and tribulations.

Serving the Lord is a **PRIVILEGE**, yet many treat it as an obligation like that of their job. Each day is an opportunity to show people that in spite of the hardships that we may face in this life, there is a joy, a peace and a blessing that comes from knowing Jesus as our Lord and Savior.

Throughout the years, I have often thought about the things that I faced as a youth. There have been many times in my life when I wondered why these things had taken place. I've thought I'm either the luckiest person in the world or the Lord allowed these things to happen to prepare me for His work in these last days.

My thoughts went back to that day as a young man, when I was almost killed while sneaking into our neighbor's field to ride his horses.

"Michael, are you alright?"

I looked up at my best friend Don, whose face was filled with fear, as he began to pull me from the spot where I had fallen and rolled over. Suddenly I heard the sound of the other horses stampeding by, over the very spot where I had fallen just a moment before.

"Man, you saved my life", I exclaimed!

"Ah, it's nothing!, anyway you would have done the same thing for me" he said.

"I know that's what friends are for!"

"Well, I think you're lucky that you didn't break your neck", he said as he helped me up off the ground.
"Why didn't you jump off that horse at the top of the hill, when you had a chance like the rest of us did? Don smiled.

"You know, you were crazy riding that horse without a saddle down the hill anyway, you could have been killed!"

"Not me!" I smiled back, "I've got nine lives!"

Through the years, I have often thought about the events of that day and what might have happened if my best friend at the time, had not pulled me out of the way of those horses. We had secretly been riding on them all afternoon. Like many young people our age, we believed we were indestructible. So, on that afternoon we decided to sneak into our neighbor's field and dare one another to ride those horses without a saddle. We believed nothing could go wrong or ever happen to us. I had watched as each of my friends would pick a horse and then jump on it bareback and ride around the field, until the horse made its way up the hill with the other horses. Then before the horse would bolt down the hill, they would each jump off, not wanting to take any chances of being hurt.

Now it was my turn! I remember picking out what seemed like the most difficult horse to ride. Then with a little help from my friends, jumped on and held on to its mane and rode around the field yelling and laughing. I thought to myself that there was nothing that I couldn't do and accomplish, if I set my mind to it. At that moment, the horse started to the top of the hill and started to bolt down the hill. It was time to jump, but I made a decision to ride it to the bottom. I had to go down that hill and make it, because no one else was willing to do it.

Let me ask you a question.

"How many times have you wanted to jump from your fears and the problems that you were facing in life. Knowing that it might be very dangerous to go on?"

It's easy to jump off when you're in a safe zone and when things are going good, but what happens when you are faced with going on and you have to make a split moment decision that will affect your life and your future. The difference between succeeding and failing in life may lie in that one moment of time when you have to make that important decision. It means taking a chance in life and taking a chance on other people. The world is filled with people who are afraid to do anything and afraid to take chances and afraid to go out on a limb.

They are afraid to step out into the unknown, where they have little or no control of the situation.

Learning to be successful in life, means learning to trust in others and learning to trust and believe in yourself, but most of all learning to trust in the Lord.

Many in the Christian walk believe that they are successful because they have never been under attack from the enemy and they have never made any serious mistakes or bad decisions. What we sometimes fail to realize, is that the Bible constantly tells us that being a Christian, is going to be a battle and not a picnic in this life, unless you're never doing anything for the Lord and then the world will leave you alone along with the devil.

James 1:12 says, "Blessed is the man that endureth temptation, for when he is tried, he shall receive the crown of life, which the Lord hath promised to them that love Him."

The word for temptation (pelrazo) is used two ways in the New Testament.

James 1:2 says, "Dear brothers, is your life full of difficulties and temptations?" "Then be happy, for when the way is rough, your patience has a chance to grow. So don't try to squirm your way out of problems. For when your patience is finally in full bloom, then you will be ready for anything, strong in character, full and complete."

I Peter 1:6,7 says, "So be truly glad! There is wonderful joy ahead, even though the going is rough for a while down here on earth." "These trials are only to test your faith, to see whether or not it is strong and pure. It is being tested as fire gets to test gold and purifies it and your faith is far more precious to God than mere gold; so if your faith remains strong after being tried in the test tube of fiery trials, it will bring you much praise and glory and honor on the day of His return."

The problem is that most of us don't believe any of that. We don't believe that the true and living God is really in control of our lives at all. Oh we always go running to him when things get so bad we don't know where else to turn. But in reality, few of us really believe that He is concerned about the everyday affairs of our lives. When in fact He is constantly making preparation for your refinement. We get so caught up in our own wants and needs and the trials that we feel we have to endure, that we just throw up our hands and assume that God doesn't really hear us or care.

Have you forgotten that it was God who created the Father and Mother image. It was Him that put that deep love and caring into the hearts of man. So, as you look at your children and desire the very best for them and go about trying to see that they get it, don't you think that the creator of your very being feels the same way about you? Fortunately for us, He knows how to cause you to be the best that you can be. Why won't we listen? Instead of throwing up our hands and saying, "I guess you can't hear me God, or you obviously don't care." Why don't we say, "I know you care God, what is it that I need to learn out of this?" In spite of all the evil in the world and the wars and violence that we've all had to endure, God is still in control. He wants to strengthen you and give you courage to accomplish all that He has put in you to do. And YOU CAN DO IT!!!

As Christians, we are going to face problems in life whether they are from the enemy or from our own mistakes. Life is not going to be just a simple walk with no mistakes and no problems. Yes, we can be blessed and we can walk in the gifts and the fruits of the Holy Spirit. But, serving Jesus means that we are going to face trials and temptations and situations in life that are going to test us each day that we live until Jesus returns. We cannot escape from these daily battles but we can become victorious through them. So you might ask yourself, if my trials are going to be so much stronger if I'm serving the Lord, then why should I? The answer is, you will miss the most incredible life you've ever known. You may think you know what's best for you, but only God knows the ultimate best. And, He only reveals it to those who will serve Him. The Bible says, "Eyes have not seen, nor ears heard, nor has entered into the heart of man the things that the Lord has prepared for those that love Him."

BLESSED BE THE NAME OF THE LORD.

You don't know real love,
Until you've known Jesus.

You haven't experienced true compassion
Until you've seen through His eyes.

And you'll never realize
Your full potential
Until you,

"Let Go, and Let God."

There will come a time unless the Lord comes first, that each of us will have to face the test of fire like the three Hebrew boys, to find out whether or not we are going to be faithful and put our complete trust in the Lord.

Those three young men were willing to believe that the God of Heaven would keep them from this horrible death and yet listen to their words found in Daniel 3:17-18:

"If it be so, our God whom we serve is able to deliver us from the burning fiery furnace, and he will deliver us out of thine hand, O King. But if not, be it known unto thee, O King, that we will not serve thy gods, nor worship the golden image which thou hast set up."

Each of us will have to make choices in the coming days and weeks that will not be popular and yet we cannot compromise our relationship with the Lord. You may be facing a fiery furnace of your own and its time that you made a decision whether or not to trust the Lord. Shadrach, Meshach and Abendego knew the God of their youth and they had never been in a place like this before yet they were willing to put God to the test. They knew that He could deliver them out of their situation, yet this wasn't the condition for their faith, because they knew that even if it meant death and even if God never delivered them out, that He was still God and that He would get the glory through the trial.

Maybe we have become too dependent on God, and therefore expect Him to get us out of every situation that we have gotten ourselves into. It's not that He can't or won't, but maybe we need to still express our faith and trust in Him, even if we have to go through the fire's of life, knowing that it may cost us everything that we have, including our lives.

One of the greatest faith builders that I have, is when I read the Old Testament and see how the hand of Almighty God came through for the people. When I'm through reading, I'm excited and overly anxious to see the God of Abraham, Isaac and Jacob perform miracles in my own life. And I'm even more assured that He will, because He loves me just like He loved them.

I have often said in our crusades, that everything we have in this life is because He gave it to us and has blessed us as we walk in obedience to His word and His promises. Maybe it's time for each of us to spend more time praising Him for what we have and where we have been in life, instead of asking Him for things of the world that we don't have as Christians.

I am often reminded of a dear pastor that I learned to respect and trust through the years. He was almost 80 years old in 1988 when I first met him and he invited me to his church and into his home. I'll never forget listening to his words of wisdom, like the disciples sitting at the feet of Jesus.

"I once had a dream", he said, "In that dream, I was taken to Heaven and stood before the gates of the city. The angel of the Lord was standing there in front of me and asked if I had anything to give unto the Lord on this day. Naturally I told him that I had done many things and suddenly another angel appeared with all of my works and I smiled at all the accomplishments that I had done through my life while on earth. Then another angel appeared and he suddenly took all of those works and threw them into a fire that had just appeared and I found myself crying, because a moment ago, they had been there for me to see, but now they were gone and burned up in a minute of time."

"As I stood there crying and weeping and wondering if I had anything to give to the Lord, another angel then appeared carrying white pearls." I heard a voice say, "This is what is left after being placed into a testing of fire and I began to rejoice, knowing that now I could stand before the Lord with my gifts and offerings."

There is coming a day, when each of us must stand in a day of judgement and our works will be put to the fire and a time of weeping or sorrow or a time of joy and rejoicing is going to take place.

I Corinthians 3:12-15 says, "Now if any man build upon this foundation of gold or silver or precious stones or wood and hay and stubble;
Every man's work shall be made manifest; for the day's shall declare it, because it shall be revealed by fire; and the fire shall try every man's work of what sort it is.
If any man's work abide, which he hath built thereupon he shall receive a reward.
If any man's work shall be burned, he shall suffer the loss, but he himself shall be saved; yet so as by fire."

Serving God will not always be easy, but it will be rewarding, not only in this life, but in the one to come. For we have a promise, that we can stand upon as Christians, knowing in a very short time that we will be going home.
Your life right now may be facing problems and trials, yet I believe that God will be able to do for you what you can't do for yourself.

For many, their life is like the man who went to work and after being on the job for a while, was hurt and wrote his boss a letter describing his condition, and asking for a leave of absence. Listen to his own words and see if the situation may not be the same in your life.

"I arrived on the job, after a storm. Immediately I began to check over the building, that we had been working on for weeks. I saw that the roof needed immediate repair. I then rigged a hoist and a boom and attached a rope in such a way to the barrel, that I could lift the bricks and pull them to the top of the building.

When I pulled the barrel to the top, I was able then to secure the rope at the bottom. And after repairing the roof, I went back and filled the barrel with left over bricks.

I then went down to the ground and released the rope to lower the bricks, but the barrel was heavier than I was and it jerked me off the ground. I was afraid to let go of the rope, so I held on and it started carrying me to the top of the building.

Halfway up, I met the barrel coming down and received a blow to the shoulder, but I still hung on. It carried me to the top of the building where I hit my head on the boom and I caught my fingers in the pulley.

In the meantime, the barrel crashed to the ground and I soon discovered that the barrel burst open and spilled bricks everywhere, thus making the barrel lighter than me and I started down at high speed.

Halfway down, I met the barrel coming up and received a blow to my shins. I however, continued down and then fell on the bricks, thus hurting myself.

At this point, I must have lost my mind, because I let go of the rope and thus released the barrel which came down a moment later and hit me on the head.

I respectfully request a leave!"

Many are in the valley of despair right now and it seems like there is no way out. Your valley is just the beginning of a mountain that the Lord wants you to climb out of during this time. But remember that you must continue to look up and discover that the Lord has a miracle for you. The reason some of us never receive our miracle, is we never believe that if we look up we'll see Him. Restoration from "SHATTERED DREAMS AND BROKEN HEARTS" only come as a result of totally giving your life over to the Lord Jesus Christ. Only then can He cause healing to come, and only then can you find true purpose for your life. When that happens, we will have the courage and strength to,

DREAM ANOTHER DREAM

CONCLUSION

It is our hope and prayer, that somewhere in the midst of reading this book, you were able to feel and see the love that God has for you.

Through all the trials and eventual triumphs in my own life, I hope it was a continual revelation to you, of God's unwavering steadfast faithfulness on our behalf.

The scriptures say that God is no respector of persons. What He will do for me, He will also do for you. Expect the Unexpected. Reach for the Unbelieveable and Soar with the pride of an Eagle.

And remember, no one loves you like Jesus does. He knows exactly where you are at all times and He continually makes intercession to Father God on your behalf.

God Bless You

Rev. Michael Shaw

EPILOGUE

As I began the task of co-writing this book with Rev. Michael Shaw, it was a tremendous opportunity for me to express my own view of how important a relationship with Jesus Christ really is. It is my deepest desire that the readers would be reminded to have compassion for other people that go through trials in this life. And realize that God is in control of every obstacle that comes our way. It is His desire to be in fellowship with us and only then can we have the confidence that He truly hears our every cry.

In my own walk with the Lord, the times that I felt the most vulnerable and less likely to be victorious, was when I failed to include Him in my everyday affairs. We must believe that "He is, and that He is the rewarder of those that diligently seek Him."

Let me encourage you to find a quiet place on a regular basis to be "Shut in with God," and I will assure you that the "King of Kings" and the "Lord of Lords" will meet you there. That's a promise, from God the Father.

My Utmost
for
HIS HIGHEST

Victoria

May I invite you to make Jesus Christ the Lord of your life, so that you too can experience the joy of salvation and victory over every area of your life?

The Bible says, "That if you will confess with your mouth the Lord Jesus, and will believe in your heart that God has raised Him from the dead, then you shall be saved. For with the heart man believes unto righteousness; and with the mouth confession is made unto salvation." Romans 10:9-10

Please pray this prayer with me and ask Jesus to come into your heart.

Jesus, I believe that You died for me and rose again on the third day. I confess to You that I am a sinner. I need Your love and forgiveness. Come into my life, forgive my sins, and give me eternal life. I confess You now as my Lord. Thank You for my salvation! I want to be everything you want me to be. Amen."

Now tell somebody what you just did - Don't ever be ashamed to tell others that Jesus is a part of your life.

We at Hope for Today would love to hear from you. Please take the time to answer the questions below so that we can rejoice with you.

_____Yes, I asked Jesus to come into my heart.

_____I understand that Restoration is something that I too deserve to have in my life, no matter what I may have done in the past.

_____I have a greater desire to have Jesus in my life after reading this inspiring story of hope and restoration.

NAME_____

ADDRESS_____

CITY/STATE/ZIP_____

Watch for Rev. Michael Shaw's
forthcoming book
in the Spring of '96
entitled,

"DREAM ANOTHER DREAM"

FOR FUTURE BOOKINGS

OR PRAYER REQUESTS

CONTACT:

HOPE FOR TODAY

REV. MICHAEL SHAW

638 BRINTON STREET

ELLSWORTH, IOWA 50075

(515) 836-4697